D0902569

Toys That Teach Your Child

From Birth to Two

Athina Aston

649.55
ast
c.1

The East Woods Press
Charlotte, North Carolina
New York   Boston

MADISON COUNTY.
CANTON PUBLIC LIBRARY SYSTEM
CANTON, MISS. 39046

Second Printing, 1985

© 1984 by Fast & McMillan, Publishers

All rights reserved. No part of this book may be reproduced without permission from the publisher, except by a reviewer who may quote brief passages in a review; nor may any part of this book be reproduced, stored in a retrieval system or transmitted in any form or by any means, electronic, mechanical, photocopying, recording or other, without permission from the publisher.

Library of Congress Cataloging in Publication Data
Aston, Athina.
 Toys that teach your child from birth to two.

 Includes index.
  1. Child development.   2. Toys.   3. Play.   4. Child rearing.   I. Title.
HQ769.A835   1984   649'.55   84-48038
 ISBN 0-88742-015-X (pbk.)

Cover photography courtesy of
Johnson & Johnson Child Development Products

Set in Palatino by Carolina Compositors, Inc., Charlotte

Printed in the U.S.A.

This East Woods Press book is available at special volume discounts for bulk purchases for sales promotions, premiums or fund raising. Special books or book excerpts can also be created to fit specific needs.

For details write the Sales Director, The East Woods Press, 429 East Boulevard, Charlotte, NC 28203.

An East Woods Press Book
Fast & McMillan Publishers, Inc.
429 East Boulevard
Charlotte, NC 28203

Contents

Introduction
Beginning a Lifelong Adventure

Having a baby is a unique event. You have added to and changed your life enormously, all at once. Never is there a beginning more moving or more momentous with possibilities than the birth of a child.

Suddenly, you hold the future in your arms. Most of your baby's life will be in the 21st century. The year 2000, once a distant gateway to the unimaginable, is just around the corner for your child. You have a new life in your family and there is a new world ahead. Here is a human being with *everything* to learn. The most important education your child will have in the next two years will be your loving attention. There are all sorts of ways you can prepare your little voyager for the excitement ahead. This early experience with you, his parents, is the crucial beginning of a long-term investment. You can expand the potential for a human being who may very well be around for a full century.

This marvelous prospect has its beginnings at birth. Now, you will be celebrating life in the most joyous way—sharing, nurturing and influencing the development of a growing child.

The immediate challenge is to understand your baby so you can begin the task of raising a happy, healthy and emotionally stable child who will grow to become a successful, competent adult. It's not impossible. Even if you aren't an experienced parent, nature and your own instinct will work with you. But, you may be asking yourself a few basic questions.

What do I really know about a baby? What does a baby see and understand and what is a baby able to do? How can I be the best parent to my child? What steps can I take to help develop my infant's full potential?

Continuing research in infant learning and child behavior is proving that babies know more than people used to think. They see more, hear more and understand more as newborns. A baby starts to learn very rapidly from the moment of birth, organizing and immediately using the acquired knowledge to propel himself forward mentally and physically. Your child's first weeks and months are critically important as a base for a future life.

Yale Psychology Professor William Kessen, who has been studying infants for more than 30 years, describes the newborn baby's energetic approach to life as "He's eating up the world."

This was not always the popular view. Traditionally, children were thought of as being boring. In medieval times infants were regarded as "unimportant, uninformed animals"; in the sixteenth century as "exasperating parasites." John Locke proclaimed it self-evident that the infant's mind was a "blank tablet" waiting to be written upon. Babies, and young children, were not seen as individuals with their own identities.

In the past, full-time parents spent much less time with their children than some working parents do today. Child-rearing practices were determined by the harsh realities of life. Tradition called for children to be swaddled and almost totally isolated from their surroundings for the first four to six months. They couldn't suck their thumbs for comfort, turn their heads or crawl. The isolation, sensory deprivation and lack of physical closeness to the mother figure often resulted in an adult who was emotionally crippled. It was only toward the end of the seventeenth century and during the eighteenth that attitudes toward children began to change.

While Victorians varied from harsh punishment to permissive treatment, by the end of the nineteenth century the child-oriented family became the standard for all classes in western society.

Lloyd deMause, researcher in the field of family history and the founder of *The Journal of Psychohistory: A Quarterly Journal of Childhood and Psychohistory*, claims that "child-rearing practices have been the central force for change in history." Family history research shows that the possessiveness and affection toward infants, which we take for granted, is a recent development. Even the maternal instinct to breast-feed one's own child was not instinctive for many women for over 1,800 years.

Today we are much more self-conscious about how we raise children, and this awareness may help us to be more thoughtful about the way we treat them.

Infant research has grown so during the past twenty years that now all major universities are devoting time to the study of the infant.

More than a decade ago, Dr. Jerome Bruner, a child psychologist and founder of the Center for Cognitive Studies at Harvard University, said, "Any subject can be taught effectively in some intellectually honest form to any child at any stage of development." Dr. Arnold Gesell, founder of the Clinic of Child Development at Yale University in 1911, has made American parents literate about the developmental stages of children. Scientists and scholars at Harvard, MIT and other universities have contributed to our awareness of the extraordinary importance of a baby's early education. These scientists have pieced together conclusive evidence that the tiniest infant is drinking in the world at a rapid pace.

It is now recognized that more than 50 percent of a child's measurable intelligence is developed before the age of five and, significantly, that a creative, stimulating environment can actually increase the child's perception and awareness as well as promote rapid growth. *The more a child sees and hears and learns, the more he wants to see and hear and learn.* According to Yale's Kessen: "The past 15 to 20 years have demonstrated that the child has a mind. The next several years will be used to find out how it works."

To take advantage of these early-learning opportunities, you need to know a good bit about your baby's growth and development and about the educational materials of all kinds that are available. In our toy and play material research, we have found that in general the products distributed by the educational toy companies such as Fisher-Price, Johnson & Johnson, Child Guidance, Little Tikes, Childcraft, Brio and others are superior. These manufacturers' toys are better conceived, better designed for wear and durability, tend to be more flexible than standard commercial toys, and offer baby multiple play opportunities. Many such toy firms have spent a great deal of time and special effort on infant development research which results in playthings that are well suited to the abilities of the infant, toddler and pre-school child. The best toys are those that can grow as the child grows. The most effective toys are those that stimulate exploration and discovery. The most interesting toys to the developing child are those which constantly present a challenge, yet allow for the successful mastery of a new skill. This is not to say that there are no useful toys manufactured by other companies, but we do urge you to send for the catalogs of the educational toy companies, look at what's available and make your own wise choice.

The early years can be a time of satisfying accomplishment and enormous fun for both parents and baby. It takes a while to explore a whole new world, and we don't promise any magical shortcuts, but we can give you a tremendous amount of useful information. We will tell you what is happening to your baby month by month and what you can do about it. You, as parents, will become the experts and will be able to greatly enrich the life of your child.

We can assure you that your baby is a unique individual right from the start with a separate personality, moods, body structure, temperament and rate of development. There is no average child in real life, and you will learn to live with your baby as he is and love him for this very individuality. If the basic needs are cared for, your child will grow and gain mastery of self just as nature intended.

What your baby needs most, of course, is all the love, care and attention you can give. *Expressed* love is the indispensable ingredient. Much of the time your child will be a delight and invite that love, but you can also expect occasions when there will be constant demands on your time, energy and patience. But what pleasure you will have when you begin to feel attuned to each other and when your infant first looks up at you and smiles, or takes that first step!

What we hope to do here is tell you what *more* you can do. We want you to know what miraculous changes are taking place inside your baby. We want you to read special signals or body language so you can respond to the child's needs. And we want to tell you about the educational products of many manufacturers that will help you make your baby's environment more exciting and enriching at each stage of development. It is, of course, simply not possible to include all the educational materials and toys available. But we hope to give you a broad representative selection of all kinds of things your baby will enjoy and learn from. It will be a great source of satisfaction to you to know how you can cooperate with your child as he grows and increasingly masters his body and his mind. With your support, he will develop his skills and reach his potential.

The importance of parental involvement in toy selection and playing cannot be stressed too strongly. The parents who participate in their child's play are best equipped to match toys to the emerging capabilities of the child. They are more aware of the right time to become involved. Parents can have their greatest influence on their children through play.

Dr. Brian Sutton-Smith, authority on child development, describes how parents contribute to a child's growth through play:

1. Parents encourage playfulness in children through example.
2. By introducing new toys and new play concepts, parents assure the progress of the play curriculum.
3. Parent-child play periods encourage imitation by children and help them to become comfortable in dealing with new situations.

The following suggestions will help parents learn more about the child and also to observe how that child is developing:

1. Through close observation, determine a child's skills level and play interests.
2. Play at the child's level. Be careful not to impose an adult play level, for it can cause disenchantment for both parent and child.
3. After a while parents can introduce a slightly newer, more complex play level.
4. Observe the child at a new task. . . . After the parents' demonstration of the new concept, they should leave the child alone to practice the new skill.

After a new skill is mastered (the process could take months or, at other times, just minutes), the parent can then participate in and applaud the child's new ability. At this time, the parent can then demonstrate another, more advanced way of using the toy. You will find that even if the child is not fully ready for another new play concept he will be stimulated by the parent's example.

In all these stages of playful interaction remember that play should be spontaneous and not forced. Never attempt to rush children through the stages of play and learning, and never try to play with a tired child.

Parental attitudes are crucial to development in play participation. Both parent and child should approach the play sessions in a spirit of fun. Play that is not fun is useless. Play that is forced or too intense, no matter how "educational" the toy, will merely make the infant or toddler lose interest and turn away.

Babies have had playthings since before the dawn of history. Primitive babies reacted to stimuli the same way infants do today. They played with their rattles (gourds filled with seeds), balls, bell toys, dolls and pull toys. And so it was for the children of ancient Greece and Rome, during the Dark Ages, the Renaissance and Victorian eras.

Children love toys. Toys are a child's tools and play is a very serious business. Why? Because play is a process vital to the mental and physical growth of a child. He grows and learns as he plays. Through play situations, the young child is able to practice skills and theories about the world. Playthings are as important to the infant and toddler as textbooks are to the student.

Formal schooling is only one of three educational systems that affect the social, intellectual, emotional and physical development of the child. The three systems are:
- The child's relationship with parents and others
- The world of play
- Formal schooling

All contribute to the formation of the child's total personality as he grows.

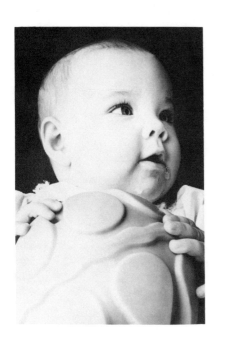

Therefore, choosing a baby's toy is as important as buying the right crib or the correct carriage. Toys teach children who they are and what they can do now and what they can become. Parents, working together with their baby, will help the child realize full potential.

Toys are the child's friends, lesson plans and the furnishings of the infant's surroundings. They have always served a vital purpose of love and companionship. The perceptive parent can gauge a child's development by observing what he delights in and what he plays with.

Your baby needs you and your encouragement every step of the way. We strongly suggest that you—the parents—become keen observers of your child's actions. Keep enthusiasm for learning alive by providing an enriched environment. Sharing this dramatic period of growth as you help your baby become a unique 'liberated' child is one of the most rewarding experiences of life. The best possible kind of nurturing or bonding, so essential to both emotional and intellectual growth, includes a combination of love and play. Nothing is as important or as much fun as playing with your baby.

Now, psychologists are urging parents to provide a stimulating and emotionally supportive atmosphere, and not to worry too much about teaching. Dr. Burton White in his book, *First Three Years of Life*, says that a balanced approach is needed during this period. "Don't concentrate on one area of development," he says. "A relaxed approach is the most effective. Laughing with, talking to and having fun (playing) is without question the best way to raise a child. Development of a child combines verbal, physical, mental, emotional and nutritional points of view."

In fact, he argues that too much pressure on your baby to learn how to speak or to solve a problem will not only slow down intellectual growth and progress but will also lead to difficulties in emotional development. "Intellectual superiority," Dr. White claims, "is very frequently obtained at the expense of progress in other areas of equal or even greater importance."

The years from birth to age two are referred to by child development experts as the sensory-motor stage of development. During this brief period, the child will experience the most rapid physical, emotional, mental and intellectual growth of his entire life. The most dramatic changes will take place during the first year.

First, the baby hears and tastes and sees. Next, he touches and feels his own body; then he explores objects outside his body. He progresses from sitting to creeping to standing. Finally, he walks! At every stage appropriate toys are needed and materials to exercise growing skills. At two months, eight months and twelve months there seem to be major periods of change in brain development, in various skills and perceptions, and in sociability.

He begins his life by being unaware of anyone existing outside himself except as a source of gratification for instinctual needs. But by the time age two is reached, a good command of the language and reaction to other people is developed. He gradually begins to "think" about concepts and how things work. He must constantly practice all these complex skills—individually and all together, and you can be crucial in helping him develop them by providing him with a wide variety of learning experiences. Always bear in mind, however, that the child has to be *free* to explore. Until your child tastes, touches, handles, sits on or falls off something, the infant can't really understand it or begin to perceive what the object is all about.

If babies could speak, perhaps their declaration of independence would be:

> "We, all babies, wish to assert our rights, too. We will not adhere to arbitrarily established schedules and routines. They're just not relevant. We reject Mommy's 'No, No's'! They stifle our curiosity. We will not compromise our physical needs for the sake of polite and civilized behavior. We are gluttonous consumers of knowledge and need boundless opportunities to learn. We feel that we can do anything. Nothing is impossible for us. We want to know, play, explore, discover and do!"

And, as each single baby seems to say in so many different ways: "I want to be me!"

For the baby under two, this independence means providing toys, objects the newborn can look at. He can feel, chew, suck, fling, bash them as he becomes a little older. And he can manipulate these objects when he is older still. Poor baby! For so many years a child was left in a crib to stare at the ceiling with nothing to challenge a ravenous curiosity about this new world. A rattle or maybe a small doll were the only tools available. This child suffered in silence.

In the early 70s, technology began to catch up, and several early learning programs were developed with the help of doctors and child study experts. Though most of the new companies survived only briefly, their impact on parents and toy manufacturers was great. The products of Dr. Burton White of Harvard (Playtentials) and the subscription program and playthings of The Learning Child were especially successful. The infant won his right to playthings geared to his special needs!

According to Dr. White, now director of the Center for Parent Education in Massachusetts, there has been an explosion in the area of infant and toddler toys. Many of the toys that are now on the market represent genuine advances over the inadequate collection that existed before. For example, once a mobile did little more than decorate the nursery. Today, toy companies—especially those active in infant research—have developed mobiles that are intelligently designed for the infant.

Increasingly, toy manufacturers are guiding parents to toys that precisely match the capabilities of children at specific ages. Companies such as Fisher-Price, Playskool, DUPLO and LEGO Systems, Johnson & Johnson, and Child Guidance have all produced playthings especially geared to infant needs and stages of development. Kiddicraft (England), Berchet (France), Dick Bruna (England), Brio (Sweden) and Brima (Portugal) are among the foreign toy firms that are creating nicely designed products in bright, primary colors.

Many toy companies now have special research and development programs. They lab-test infants and their parents under the direction of professional consultants to gauge the appeal and determine the best qualities of a toy. Some toys may be abused and battered for two or more years before they are allowed on the shelf. They are dropped down stairs, tipped off tables, twisted and 'tortured'; they are tested for chewable colors, rough edges, strength and flammability. Color and design are just as important as durability. The final result of all this input is reflected in the number of well-thought-out toys on the market for infants and toddlers.

The better conceived and more flexible toys of today offer the child the best in play value. We have identified a handful of toy companies that have been providing quality playthings for a number of years. We urge you to take a look at what is available, carefully read package directions and age recommendations before making a decision to buy. There are several interesting toy catalogs also available which feature some items not found in the usual retail outlets. Toys to Grow On, Discovery Toys, Childcraft and the classic F.A.O. Schwarz are worthwhile catalogs to explore.

It is estimated that some nine billion dollars worth of toys are sold in the United States annually. When you examine a sampling you will find that a great deal of this money is spent on toys without real play value for the very young child. We hope to help you make a more careful selection for your child's sake.

You will probably want to begin learning more about baby care long before your child's arrival. In addition to Dr. Benjamin Spock's famous book, *Baby and Child Care*, you might wish to obtain *A Child Is Born*, a collection of unbelievable photos of an unborn child; *Beginning Together*, a diary of discovery for parent and baby, by Rochelle Mayer, Ed.D.; *Your Child's First Year* by Dr. Lee Salk and *Infants and Mothers* by T. Berry Brazelton, M.D.

Also helpful are the *Better Homes and Gardens Baby Book* and *Infant Care* published by the Children's Bureau in Washington, D.C. There are many informative and useful pamphlets available through The American Academy of Pediatrics about accident and poison prevention. (At the end of this book you will find a more complete bibliography.)

Most mothers, however, will not have the time or the inclination to study the more scientific literature on child development, and that is where this publication comes in. The growth pattern of a normal child is very predictable, and there are only slight variations in the timing of the individual child's readiness to begin a new phase. You can, with a little help, easily learn what to expect your child to do, when your child will probably do it and how you can help.

> From birth to three months, the infant stabilizes his breathing, heartbeat and digestion. He learns to hold his head up; he develops the muscles of his eyes, enabling him to focus; and he bats at objects with his hands.
>
> From three to six months, he learns to reach for objects, grasp them and let go. He can roll over and sit with support.
>
> From six to nine months, he can sit alone and begins to extend muscle control to the legs and feet, enabling him to creep. He uses the thumb and forefinger in a pincer-like movement. Toward the end of this period he can place objects generally where he wants them.
>
> From nine months to one year, he creeps, pulls himself up to a standing position and lowers himself down. Forefingers are used to poke and prod.
>
> Between one and one-and-a-half years, he stands and cruises, holding on to either a person or furniture, and begins to walk. By the end of this period he can say words, a few phrases and can usually walk alone.
>
> Between one-and-a-half and two, he learns to walk well and run, and begins a more active exploration of his environment. By the end of this period he begins to acquire bowel and bladder control; is developing real language ability; and he is beginning to have a sense of personal identity.

As the baby reaches each of these developmental milestones, there are appropriate playthings that help him practice his growing skills.

Because your baby's learning and development begin from the very moment of birth, there are a few preparations you may want to make before the arrival.

One of the first items you will be thinking about is a crib for your new baby. Safety is an important consideration when buying any baby furnishings. *Consumer Reports* in their *Guide to Buying for Babies* finds that crib accidents account for 50,000 injuries each year. Many accidents occur when the infant's head is caught between the crib slats or in the gap between mattress and crib sides. Now, mandatory government standards rule that the maximum distance between slats be no more than two and three-eighths inches, a space far too small for a baby's head to pass through. The interior crib dimensions are also standardized by law so that a regular crib mattress will fit snugly, leaving no hazardous gap.

Mesh cribs have proven to be dangerous because your baby can become caught in the net.

What about diapers, high chairs, baby carriages, car restraints, add-on bike seats? Which is safest? Which a good buy? *Guide to Buying for Babies* brings together reliable information on the great variety of baby products on the market with a special eye to their safety.

The following books offer advice on the numerous baby products on the market: *Good Things for Babies* by Sandy Jones; *The Whole Child: A Sourcebook* by Stevanne Auerbach, Ph.D. and *The Ultimate Baby Catalog* by Michele Ingrassia Haber and Barbara Kantrowitz.

There are two other items to consider now that may seem like gifts for you, but, as you will see, are really for the baby. You will need a camera so that you can keep your own visual record of your baby's growth and activities. Your camera should be equipped to take indoor shots and close-ups. It should be easy to operate so that picture-taking does not become a complicated process, but is something so routine to you and your baby that it can be accomplished quickly and unobtrusively. If you have to wait to make many adjustments, the spontaneity of the moment will have passed before you are ready. You will find, especially when your baby is older, that he will tend to pose when he realizes you are about to snap.

So, get a simple, easy-to-operate camera and take it to the hospital with you. Your roommate can take pictures of you with your baby, and you can do the same for her. Color film isn't necessary for this kind of record; you can take many more black-and-white pictures for the same cost. If you use a fast black-and-white film, you can take most indoor pictures without flash bulbs if there is a reasonable amount of light. A window may provide the illumination you need, or you can take the shade off the lamp.

Not only will your candid snapshots rekindle memories of your baby that you might otherwise forget, but they will also be treasured by your child in a few more years. When he is ready for picture books, what could be more exciting than a picture book of *him*? There is a stage when children become very curious about themselves as babies (this often occurs when the next child is born); what could be better than showing him what he looked like and what he did when he was a baby? And when an older child is cranky or sad or sick in bed, there is nothing quite so comforting as a personal photo album.

Movie and video cameras are becoming less expensive all the time. More and more families can enjoy having their own home movies as a record of these precious years.

The last item you need is a really good baby book. *Our Baby's First Seven Years*, produced by the Mother's Aid of the Chicago Lying-In Hospital at the University of Chicago, is especially good and is available in large bookstores (a small bookstore will order it for you). It provides space for recording details of the infant's mental, physical and social development, including such items as eye and visual development, progress in speech and hearing, eating and sleeping habits, development of independence, medical history and immunizations, and a wealth of information that is not only interesting, but may at some time prove to be vital.

There is also room in this book for things the child will enjoy in later years—pictures before and after his first haircut, photographic records of birthday parties, gifts received, data about school and early playmates, samples of first printing and handwriting, etc. It costs no more than run-of-the-mill record books, and it's nice to know that the profits help support maternity research at the hospital.

[You no doubt have noticed already that we have referred to your child as "he." Of course we are dealing with both boys and girls. But for the sake of convenience we are, in accord with tradition, using the pronoun "he" throughout the general discussion. There is no sex discrimination implied and, although girls tend to develop slightly faster than boys, the developmental patterns of both sexes are remarkably alike through the early years.]

You must always bear safety in mind in choosing anything for your child. Be particularly careful to babyproof your home so that it is an inviting place for your child to explore safely. He will soon be into *everything!*

There are several safety latches often available in supermarkets, that are easily installed on wood or metal cabinets or drawers. Basically, the catch consists of a flexible hook and stop that prevents a cabinet or drawer from being pulled open more than an inch. In order to release

SMALL PARTS TEST
Any toy or part of a toy that can be detached and is intended for children under three years of age must undergo the Small Parts Test. The object is placed in a cylinder which simulates a young child's throat. The depth of entry determines age recommendations. Anything which fits entirely within the cylinder should not get into the hands of those under age three! Many other tests are used before products are approved. Toy Manufacturers' safety efforts must go hand-in-hand with responsible adult supervision.
Photo courtesy of Toy Manufacturers of America.

the catch, it is necessary to determine how it works, and then depress the hook with a finger until it disengages from the stop (something your baby can't manage yet!). Closing the door or drawer automatically resets the latch.

Be careful to keep all objects out of reach that are dangerous when broken or that your baby might swallow. Electrical cords should be kept out of the way and electrical outlets covered.

As for toys, they must be too large to swallow, must not have rough edges or sharp points that might injure the baby. Check all toys carefully for small, loose parts that could be pulled off and popped into the mouth. Button eyes on dolls or removable whistles in squeeze toys are very common hazards. Wooden toys should be sturdy and smoothly polished. Be careful to check all painted objects, toys or furniture, to make certain the paint is non-toxic. Remember, *everything* will go directly into your baby's mouth for a time!

Today's toys are designed to be safe. However, the toys that are properly matched to the child's age and ability are considered safest. Be selective whenever you buy a toy. Before you buy:

- Inspect the package for play-use and safety messages.
- Select the proper toy for the skills of each age level. Toys for older children can be too complex and, potentially, dangerous for very young children.

The Play Chart which appears in the Appendix of this guide matches types of toys with developmental stages according to age. You will also find the Safety Checklist in the Appendix useful in selecting toys for your baby.

For additional information on toy safety, we suggest *Toys That Don't Care* by Edward M. Swartz, published by Gambit. It should be available at your local library. Current information on toy safety and reports on hazardous toys are also published periodically in *Consumer Reports* magazine.

What you buy for your child will depend, of course, on your family's pocketbook. You can certainly use your own imagination in converting familiar household items into playthings once you know the basic principles of the child's development and what he needs at a specific time. Improvised toys will give your baby hours of fun at little or no expense.

You should select appropriate toys. Parents should not give a child a toy he will "grow into" or expect him to play with an outgrown one any more than they would expect him to wear shoes that are not the right size. There is an important distinction between the toy that is too advanced and the toy that is a challenge. One is frustrating; the other is an incentive to exert a little more effort. Notice the age indicated on the toy, but use your own judgment about a toy's suitability for your child.

The size of the toy is often an important consideration, regardless of the age grouping. A ball should be manageable. The child should be able to handle the pieces of a puzzle. The stuffed animal should be of dimensions that allow the child to carry it around handily.

In general, if the toys you have are no longer a challenge to a child, new ones should be introduced to enhance the next step in development.

Try to balance the toys you purchase so that your baby can practice all newly acquired skills as he goes along. During the next two years your baby will be playing with toys in these categories:

- Ball—soft, plush or rubber
- Bath Toy—a floating animal or fish, boat, pouring containers
- Cuddly Companion—a bear or other animal, doll or story book character
- Musical Toy—to listen to
- Noisemaking Toy—to shake, to bang or pound
- Books and Records—about familiar objects surrounding baby
- Building Toys—take apart-put together items to challenge young hands and fingers
- Shape Sorter—to help baby discriminate between colors and shapes
- Wheeled Toys—cars, push-pull alongs, carriages
- Imitative Grown-up Toys—all the "real life" toys, pots, pans, clothes, that tell baby he is part of your world
- Wheeled Ride-on Toys—walkers and riding toys

It is true that the more beautiful and exciting the objects are that you work with together, the more fun your baby's world will be for him and for you. Your child will move from one stage of development to another when *he* is ready. He will let you know his desire to begin to test a new skill. You cannot push him or expect too much of him. The more patience you have with him, the better. Sometimes he will fail and be frustrated; sometimes you will be disappointed in his slowness. Knowing what to expect and what you can do for your baby will help make your home a happier place and early life more productive. We hope we can help you get started with your child in the wonderful adventure of life.

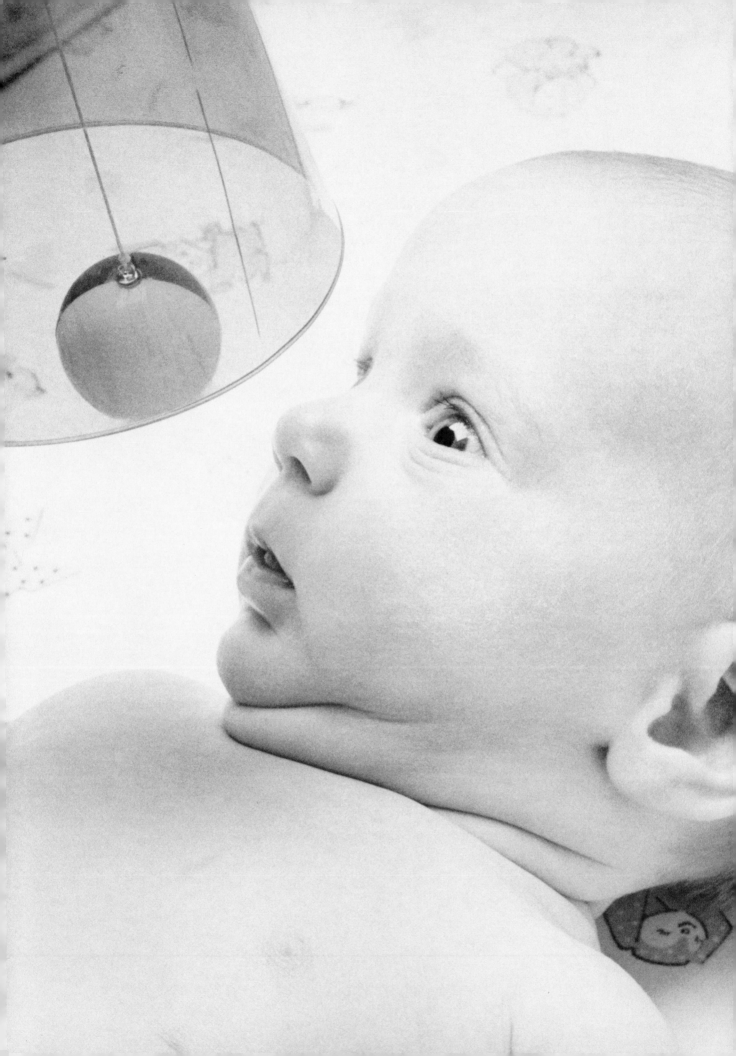

Newborn to Three Months
Sound and Light

Suddenly, after these long months of waiting you find yourself home at last with your beautiful baby. It is important that the entire family stop for a moment and take a look at personal and household schedules. Many adult-centered, and leisure-time activities may have to accommodate themselves to the new baby's schedule. Sleeping late on a Sunday morning—or sleeping throughout the night for that matter—may be a luxury you will have to give up for a short while. It is important for the mother to be able to relax, get some extra rest and take extra care of herself at this time. The physical and emotional changes of the past nine months require that she get special attention during these first few months.

All the family's energies will be concentrated on learning about the temperament and needs of this wonderful and exciting (but very demanding) new member. From the very beginning you will see considerable activity taking place in your baby's growth and learning. You will want to be physically and mentally ready to help your child in every way you can.

Set up a schedule in which both mother and father can share in the caring of the baby. A child who has the loving support of both parents right from the start has a distinct advantage over the baby who may have only his mother to look after him.

From continuing research it is more and more evident that the father's influence on a child begins in infancy. These studies have shown that fathers who are exposed to their children during the very first hours of life generally demonstrate a more enthusiastic attachment to their newborns.

The father's participation in the care of an infant contributes a great deal to the child's development. The child becomes socially more responsive and eventually tests higher when the father is involved in child care.

One study conducted by the National Institute of Child Health and Human Development showed that the more active fathers were with their children, the higher the five to six month old infants scored on the Bayley Mental Development Index, a test that measures a baby's cognitive and motor skills. It was also found that infants whose fathers frequently bathed and dressed them withstood stress better than infants whose fathers didn't do as many of the caretaking tasks such as bathing, changing, dressing and feeding.

Another well-known study by Dr. Michael Yogman and his associates at the Boston Children's Medical Center videotaped the weekly interactions of infants and each of their parents. The two to three minute sessions began when the baby was two weeks old and were conducted over a period of six months. In each session, each parent was asked to *play* with the baby without using props. The fathers were more likely to engage in accentuated rhythmic play—hence more physical play. Mothers were more likely to engage in verbal exchanges, with baby cooing and the mother imitating the child's sounds and facial expressions. The fathers, therefore, proved to be more vigorous; the mothers tended to handle the infant smoothly and gently.

But, the most significant discovery from the infant behavior studies is that the father is no longer the forgotten contributor to a child's development. His interaction with his son or daughter does make a difference!

The most important job both parents will have during the first few months of a child's life is building trust. Remember, the baby, now almost totally helpless, must feel that the world around him is reliable and that all his needs will be met. There are several ways in which a parent can build this trust:

1. Respond to his needs—you really cannot spoil a baby.
2. Communicate with him—your baby will love the sound of your voice. Speak in a soft, gentle manner. Smile, laugh, sing and play with him.
3. Touch the infant—hold and hug him. He loves being cuddled.

All these natural and usually automatic parental responses greatly help to build self-esteem in the infant that will last a lifetime.

There will be so many *firsts* during the first twelve months (first smile, sitting up, crawling, talking, scribbling, walking). Your enthusiastic and positive reaction will reinforce baby's pride in having learned a new skill or made a new discovery about himself and his surroundings.

Everything should be done to encourage the baby's insatiable curiosity. Don't forget, biologically your child *MUST* seek out new experiences. Your toddler *MUST* acquire new knowledge, and *MUST* explore!

It seems, according to all the data gathered by infant researchers, that the kind of experience a child receives in the first few years of life plays an important role in total development. The child who has a warm, loving relationship with parents and family and who lives in interesting surroundings with many opportunities to interact with others has the best chance to become a competent adult. Providing the child with such an environment as well as with *RESPONSIVE* playthings is one of the challenges of parenting.

During his first weeks your baby will exist in a kind of twilight zone, sleeping perhaps twenty hours a day. The needs will be primarily physical ones. Food, warmth, cleanliness will be required, but along with these he will need a great deal of attention and affection. As Dr. Lee Salk and Rita Kramer write in their excellent guide to the emotional health of children, *How to Raise a Human Being*, "Want and need are inseparable at the earliest stages of development." The infant needs the security of knowing demands will be satisfied and that you will always be there when needed. His trust in you is crucial, his whole approach to life and his future relationships with people depend upon it. Remember, he is a newcomer to the cold, outside world, and it must seem very foreign to him after those nine months of gestation. So at this very early stage, paradise will consist of being wrapped warmly, held securely, kept clean and comfortable, and fed when hungry.

At birth and during the first weeks, your child's most active area will be the mouth. The baby is born with a strong sucking instinct and a rooting reflex—even a light touch on his lips will start them moving. His very sensitive mouth is the center of his being, and his greatest pleasure will be the breast or the bottle. Even when not nursing, his lips will open and close searchingly. He is already "learning" what to expect from the world. If his hunger cries bring prompt feeding, he learns that he can influence his environment. This provides the foundation for a healthy self-confidence.

Arriving at a comfortable, mutually convenient schedule of feeding will be your most pressing task. Babies' temperaments vary greatly in this regard. Some will adapt almost immediately to a regular routine, whereas others will take a longer time. In either case, your baby is sure to be insistent in his demands—that angry, red face and shrill cry trumpet a desperate need for food. *Now!* Experts today believe that letting the infant lead the way in setting up his own routine is the best plan. Referred to as the 'demand' schedule, this simply means your baby should be fed when hungry and not forced to lie awake at odd hours (or stalled off) in accord with a rigid feeding schedule. He follows his own internal rhythm.

In all probability, your child will soon settle into a fairly stabilized pattern that you can adapt to the family routine. Whatever timing works best for you both is the answer. Once a schedule is established, try to follow it as regularly as possible.

During these first weeks your baby's bodily functions may be somewhat erratic. He may breathe irregularly and have startle reactions, lashing out with his arms and legs. He can turn his head to the center line, but in general he will assume a characteristic pose known as the tonic neck reflex. His head will be turned to one preferred side, the arm on that side extended and the other arm flexed. His fingers will remain clenched in a tight fist. His neck muscles are not strong enough now to support his heavy head, and it will bob about if not firmly supported.

Until very recently, almost everyone has assumed that the newborn baby was relatively unaware of his surroundings and that he was content simply to eat and sleep. New research indicates that babies are much more alert to their surroundings than had been suspected. They are actively drinking in impressions and registering sights and sounds. Dr. Jerome Bruner has coined the expression, "Babies are smarter than you think." He and his research staff have established that even on the day of birth, infants can distinguish diagonal lines from checkerboard patterns and can follow an object with their eyes that is moved within their area of vision for a short distance.

All of your baby's senses mature continuously from the moment of birth. But, during the first two months of life, the coordination and focus of your baby's eyes will be the most important phase of development. His first exploration of the world around him will be through his eyes. During the first month, his general vision will be dim. A baby is born with a rudimentary sense of vision (20/500). He will seem to stare vacantly into the distance at windows, the ceiling, at people. However, your baby *CAN* see light and shadow and shape, and within a few months the six pairs of tiny eye muscles that control focusing gradually come under control.

FIRST TOYS

The newborn begins by looking at the edges of things. Even before he is able to bring objects into focus, there is a clear area of vision that is about eight to twelve inches from the face. At eight weeks a baby can differentiate between shapes of objects as well as colors. Babies generally prefer red, then blue or yellow. Hence, these are the primary colors used for infant toys. At three months the infant begins to develop stereoscopic vision. As he grows he focuses more and more on his mother's face—usually at this stage the main source of his comfort.

What your baby needs during these early weeks and months is a variety of things to look at, both near and far. The child is able to see patterns of light and dark and will be fascinated by sunlight streaming in windows, tree boughs swaying outside the window or shadows reflected on the ceiling and walls. Sometimes a fretful baby will be quieted simply by turning on the lamp in the room. You can provide your baby with a glowing animal night lamp or a night light that plugs directly into the electrical outlet or a set of twinkling mini-lights.

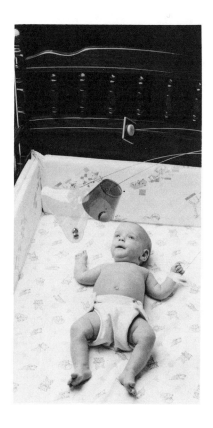

When you are furnishing and decorating your newborn's room, keep in mind that babies are more interested in looking at bright strong colors and patterns than at the traditional pastel pinks and blues. Remember too that in several months your baby will be eagerly exa- mining every part of the room with his eyes. Then the child will enjoy patterned curtains, brightly colored pictures and posters, and, perhaps, a vivid rug on the floor. (The rug needs to be soft, since a great deal of time will soon be spent playing there.)

A crib bumper protects your baby's head from the crib bars but also, unfortunately, prevents him from seeing out. Try to find a clear vinyl bumper that can be seen through. Some of these have abstract designs and patterns which will intrigue your child.

Because he sees best within that area eight to twelve inches from his face, he needs bright, colorful, moving objects near him that he can observe.

Two very lovely, stylized human figures designed by Antonio Vitali are appropriate as baby's first toys. The brightly colored, smooth wood "touch me" figures can be suspended from the side of his crib and he will turn his head to gaze at them. The real people standing by his crib making those ooo-ing and ahhh-ing sounds are still shadowy blurs.

From the very first moments of his birth, your baby is keenly aware of sound. A baby's ears function even before he is born, so a newborn arrives with a whole set of auditory reactions. A newborn can localize a sound ten minutes after birth! He can also distinguish pitch and is more responsive to a high pitched voice than to a low pitched one. If you give a baby a choice between a male voice and a female voice, he will turn to the the female voice. Even a three-day-old infant can pick out the mother's voice. He will associate it with comfort, feeding, warmth and the satisfaction of his most basic needs. Your baby loves the soothing timbre of your voice, so speak to him from the very start. If dad doesn't get a smile or reaction when he tries, don't be discour- aged. Child study experts found that when fathers pitched their voices slightly higher the infants immediately responded.

In these next few months, the baby will begin to turn toward familiar voices and will begin to imitate voice inflections. Infants from four to six months old have the ability to sense and imitate variations in pitch with surprising accuracy. Since at this age mother means business (feeding) to the baby, your child will gravitate to the mother. A tiny baby still feels a part of her—her sounds and actions are the baby's sounds and actions.

Scientists have found that an infant's pulse rate and breathing become more regular when rhythmic soft music is played. They have speculated that these rhythmic sounds remind the child of the mother's heartbeat—range of the human heartbeat is roughly between 50 to 150 beats per minute—so familiar to the infant from life in the womb. Research has shown that as early as the third month of gestation a fetus may begin to react to external sound stimuli by moving and by changing its heart rate. Mothers have reported that during later months of pregnancy they could feel their babies responding to music.

During the next few months a baby will demonstrate an awareness of musical sounds by turning toward the source of the music. When a baby is crying, he is expressing himself in a variety of pitches and rhythms. Experiments with gurgling sounds and cooing and babbling are merely rehearsals for the day when the first word is pronounced.

You might consider putting a radio tuned to soft music near your baby's crib to soothe him. Other rhythmic sounds which may be appealing are a loudly ticking clock or a metronome. Observe your baby and see if these sounds interest and quiet him.

By the second month, your baby will begin to have more control over his bodily movements, and he will be able to hold his head erect for a short period of time. Most delightful of all, he will begin to react to any attention and will babble and coo with pleasure when you bathe and feed him. He is taking an increasingly active part in the world around him. He lies awake for longer periods of time and responds with increasing enthusiasm to both visual and aural stimuli. After the first four weeks, his random eye movements begin to come under control—he is able to align his eyes and can increasingly focus them on objects nearby. This is a great milestone in his development, for he is now able to see *what* objects are as well as *where* they are. Bear in mind that the more he sees, the more he will *want* to see.

You will now want to think about what other specific aids you can provide to stimulate your baby's eye development. It is interesting to realize that his own hand is the object he most frequently looks at and that it is just the right distance from his eyes to practice focusing on. Some scientists have speculated that this is nature's way of insuring that a baby realizes that his hand is a part of him—the first step in self-identity.

MOBILES

During these first months, when your baby is not being fed, bathed or fondled, he will spend most of his time in the crib. So you will want to make his small crib world as pleasant as possible. A mobile is the best way to provide your child with bright moving objects that dangle over his crib, twirl in the breeze and, perhaps, make a pleasing sound.

There are many excellent mobiles available, with and without music boxes. When you make your selection, keep in mind that you need to hang the mobile *near* a baby of this age—preferably from twelve inches to two feet away from his face, so that he can really see it.

The most interesting thing about a mobile to your baby is the movement of the shapes. Pick a light mobile so the slightest breeze, even the shifting weight of your tiny baby in his crib, will cause the shapes to waft and sway, bounce, turn, shimmer and produce fascinating patterns for him to look at. Pick a mobile with shapes that are feather light and cannot hurt him if he accidentally hits them with his hands or a part falls on him. Remember, too, that he sees them from below.

HAPPY FACES MOBILE
Aarikka

Generally available are the simpler mobiles consisting of a dowel stick from which fish, birds, butterflies and the like hang on strings. The hanging shapes are made of paper, plastic, cloth or wood, but unless the wood is extremely light it is best to stick with the other materials.

• AARIKKA makes a wooden mobile that is safe and pleasant for your baby. The *Happy Faces Mobile*, available from Scancraft, holds five colorful faces and promotes early focusing.

Many mobiles have music boxes or tinkling bells, and the soft, repeated musical sounds have a quieting effect. They also give the baby an opportunity to associate sounds with the visual image producing them—just as he learns to turn his head to look at you when he hears your step.

Several educational toy firms carry mobiles which sound very much like oriental wind chimes. The softest breeze sets their small wooden balls, pipes or brass chimes in motion. Glass chimes and iridescent mobiles can be found in shops specializing in Japanese imports, but since they are not designed specifically for babies, examine them for materials that may be dangerous. Most of these should not be hung directly over the crib.

There are many more complicated kinds of mobiles available:
• EDEN's *Giraffe, Clown* or *Lamb Mobile* is a striking carousel with

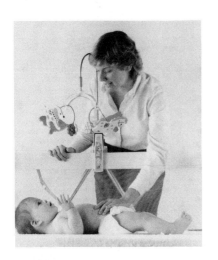

DANCING ANIMALS
MUSIC BOX MOBILE
Fisher-Price Toys

five figures revolving to the sound of soft music. These crib companions are soft to touch, and the figures can later be detached from their strings and used as play toys.

• The FISHER-PRICE *Dancing Animals Music Box Mobile* offers brightly colored animals (made of soft vinyl) which gently rock on a balancing arm to Brahms' "Lullaby." This mobile is easy to clamp to the side of the crib and plays for ten minutes.

• PLAYSKOOL makes a *Bright Skies* wall mobile of six colorful birds, bees and butterflies swirling around a rainbow. The figures are angled so that the baby's eyes can easily follow them as they dance around.

• CHILD GUIDANCE's mobile which also plays Brahms' "Lullaby" features favorite Disney characters—Mickey, Minnie, Donald and Dumbo.

These mobiles are meant to be seen as opposed to a crib gym which baby can also touch. The best mobiles are set to one side and flutter in the breeze so that your baby's eyes can play with them. (Note: As soon as your baby can reach out and touch the mobile, replace it with a crib gym. The mobile can be moved to another part of the room.)

You can also use your imagination and make your own mobiles. They can be made very simply by threading ribbon through lightweight objects, such as an unbreakable Christmas ornament or foil paper shapes. There are several patterns available for making cloth mobiles in a variety of shapes. McCall's Patterns or Simplicity have a selection of easy-to-sew mobiles. One idea that is a bit different is the sachet mobile. Follow pattern directions and be sure to leave a slot open so you can fill it with potpourri. But, always remember to check out every object you hang over a baby's crib or carriage. Make sure the objects are secure and cannot fall and would not be dangerous if they did. Make sure that the mobile is out of reach.

However, as interesting as you make the crib you don't want all your baby's time to be spent there. In fact, when he is in his crib turn him over on to his stomach several times a day. A baby needs a change of scenery as much as parents do.

An infant seat is indispensable. The baby can be strapped securely and moved to whatever room you are in. The child will enjoy your company as well as the new surroundings.

During the past decades, baby slings have come into their own and achieved the wide popularity they deserve. These baby carriers are slings or papoose-like seats with straps enabling you to carry your infant either on your back or on your chest while you make your daily rounds straightening up the house or going to market.

Many of these slings support your baby's head so that they can be used from the earliest weeks. The Snugli, designed by a former Peace

Corps nurse and based on the back packs used by African mothers, is handmade with ingenious tucks that can be let out as the baby grows. The price is high, about $45.00, but so is the value. Parents who have used Snugli are enthusiastic boosters, and *Consumer Reports* ranks it number one.

Other excellent baby carriers are generally available in department stores carrying baby furniture.

With any soft carriers, we suggest that when your baby is tiny you carry him in front, cuddled in your arms so that he can look up at you. Then, when he is three or four months old, you can let him ride with legs astride your hip.

Once your baby can hold himself erect at about six months, look for a carrier that will be the most comfortable for you and baby and enjoy the closeness of having your child very near you as you go about your chores.

Your voice is still the most important sound to your baby, soothing him when he is upset, lulling him to sleep. But you might also consider having on hand some pleasant lullaby records such as the *Golden Slumbers Soundbook* (Caedmon) or calm instrumental and orchestral works to play for him. If you have a tape or cassette recorder, you can record your own voice—or his!—for him to listen to.

By the time your baby is approaching three months of age, his eyes can follow a moving object over a considerable distance, and he turns his head to hear speaking voices. To give your child practice in finding and following sights and sounds, move things around from time to time. Stand behind your baby and talk or sing. Ring a tinkling bell below him when he is sitting on your lap. Slowly move a flashlight (dimmed with colored cellophane) back and forth and up and down across his field of vision. Sometimes start behind him, out of range of his vision, and see how soon he realizes there is something new coming into view. In short, give your baby as much as possible to look at and listen to during these first few months.

SOFT TOYS

Even the very tiny baby needs to have some soft, cuddly, "security" toys around in the crib. He won't, of course, hold them or play with them as yet, but snuggly animal and doll companions will interest him, comfort him and soon be a necessity. They appeal to your child's sense of touch, and some will, undoubtedly, end up being personal playthings for many months (or years) to come.

The baby's response to the doll is triggered by its resemblance to the human figures surrounding him. He recognizes the similar facial pattern. Dr. Brazelton observes, "Even a newborn baby, if presented with a drawing of a face, will fix his attention on it for minutes on end.

But when presented with a real human face, the infant rejects the drawing and studies the human face out of preference. At one month a baby not only recognizes the mother's face but prefers it to others."

As the baby picks up his doll he will smile and immediately "talk" to it. His cooing and babbling express pleasure with this new found companion. As he grows he will taste it, finger the doll and even energetically swing it around. The doll will be passed from hand to hand as he plays with it.

Most certainly this favorite object of baby's affections will be rudely thrown out of the crib within the next few months to test its tenacity. But, the doll always passes these loving tests. Eventually the doll takes on a definite personality and will be given a name of its own. "Knowledge is lacking in the infant, understanding has not yet begun; but wants and wishes, fears and angers, love and hate are there from the beginning." (*Nursery Years* by Susan Isaacs)

There is a greater variety of animals and dolls on the market than of any other genre of toy. Among them are old-fashioned teddy bears, simple cloth or rag dolls, and the multitude of plush or woolly puppies, bunnies, bears, lambs, etc., we all remember from our own childhood. Now we can also choose from a new selection of friends—Koala bears, Snoopy dogs and Snoopy Baby, Disney characters, and the newest soft rattles. Pick a few you feel your baby will enjoy, making sure that you select non-allergenic, soft, washable, well-stitched dolls with no removable parts.

• JOHNSON & JOHNSON's *Sailor Bear* suits baby's discovery ritual perfectly. Sailor Bear has been designed with all the special features the infant "looks for" in his first doll—something that can be hugged, grasped, squeezed, tugged at, chewed on, tossed about, and soft to touch and cuddle. Sailor Bear's hat and life preserver double as teethers. As baby plays with the doll it rattles in response to all this loving care.

• Another first doll is *Jolly Dolly* in both boy and girl shapes with embroidered faces. This doll is very lightweight and soft so that the infant can hold it easily, and it is also available in such toy catalogs as *Growing Child* and *Toys to Grow On*.

• GUND and DAKIN both have popular collections of soft and cuddly toys. The *Baby Gund* selection has been designed for the infant of this age group in appealing animal shapes.

• FISHER-PRICE offers the infant and baby a whole selection of soft dolls including the new soft rattle. *Soft Shakes* combines the two elements that a baby likes—a rattle sound within a smiling face. A Clown, Bunny or Puppy face sits upon a plump body wrapped in a calico type pattern.

SOFT SHAKES ASSORTMENT
Fisher-Price Toys

• THE FIRST YEARS also offers a soft rattle—baby's *First Teddy*.

• PLAYSKOOL's *Play Pets* (frog and teddy) contain squeakers inside soft, stuffed bodies.

These soft rattles show your baby that he can make something happen all on his own since they respond to his touch. Remember, at this time he is sorting out who he is in relation to the people and things around him. As your child explores the mouth, face and other parts of his body with his hands, he begins to distinguish among the various members of the family caring for him.

All children love the comforting toy. Many a first doll or stuffed animal winds up on the teen-ager's bed. A doll quickly becomes the child's companion, an extension of self, a substitute for mother. A soft toy that can be held and hugged makes your baby feel secure as he drifts off to sleep. The doll means more than any other toy to the child. And, he is merely carrying out a ritual that began 5,000 years ago. The appeal in the soft or rag doll is that it says "touch me and hug me." Now it's your baby's turn to cuddle and hug and love.

In these early months, the world your child inhabits is limited by the secure confines of a warm bed and your loving arms. He hasn't mastered the concept of where he himself ends and the world begins as yet, but he sees shapes, color and movement and is very aware of sounds. He needs a lot of quiet security—which only you can provide. Surround your child with a variety of bright, colorful objects to look at, pleasant sounds to soothe and give all the care and love he needs so much. You will be doing a great deal to make the first months of your baby's life exciting days of discovery, and you will be demonstrating to him that the world is a good and interesting place in which to live.

PLAY PETS
Playskool

Three to Six Months
Reaching Out to Touch

Sometime between eight and twelve weeks, you will be rewarded by the thrilling experience of your baby's first real smile. And when he enters his third month, you will begin to see definite signs of his growing desire to become a part of the world around him. Each day will bring your child more awareness of his environment, and it will be your responsibility to make the surroundings rich and tempting for exploration.

During the first three months he has been reaching out primarily with his *eyes* and *ears*, but in the three months ahead he will begin to explore with his *hands*. His eyes focus well now, and he is on the way toward coordinating hand and arm movements with what he sees. He has been watching the random movements of his hands for some time, and now he begins to play with them, touching one to the other, feeling the texture of his skin.

In the early months he had no understanding of where he stopped and the outside world began. As he experiments with his hands, he has a dawning awareness that his hands belong to him, that he exists apart from the outside world. Now he wants to touch, feel, taste and smell everything he can get his hands on. Simple groping will slowly give way to active reaching. During these next three months your child will look at the toy dangling above, reach out and touch it, and finally he will be able to make his hand move to just the spot he wants. At first he will bat at an object using his hand as a paw. Then he will close in on the object crudely with two hands. Gradually he will be able to grasp an object and close one hand around it. Still later, he will learn to open his hand and release the object.

31

The baby is now beginning to blossom. As a three-month-old he adds another dimension to his learning process. His hands suddenly come ALIVE!

During the past few months the baby has been studying his hands in every detail. He did not realize that these waving objects were a part of him, basically because he could not control them. Sometimes they merely flashed in front of him. What they were the baby did not really know.

As the infant's visual system matures, he learns how to control his reach with his eyes—achieving what psychologists call eye-hand coordination. Parents' faces, mobiles and other visual stimulation have been helping him reach the first of a number of physical milestones. All the exploring that has been going on with his eyes will now be done with his hands as well. The beginnings of prehension (visually directed reaching) indicates the gradual discovery of "self" as being separate from the rest of the world. According to infant researchers, the infant eventually realizes during play that the object (a rattle) is distinct from the action (grasping).

What is happening in the development of the infant as he learns how to reach, how to grasp for nearby objects? While lying on his back, he may accidentally find and hold the rattle in a reflex grasp (his hand instinctively closes about any object put into it), but is unable to let go of it at will.

Next, in about a month, he is not only able to grip an object, but he can also wave it over his head and in front of his eyes. He fingers the toy to study texture and composition. He reaches for and grasps the rattle; he transfers it from one hand to the other; then releases it *at will* when he tires of it. The pattern of investigation begins: grasp . . . explore . . . transfer . . . into the mouth for further evaluation. Then begin again! The baby discovers that he can enjoy the properties of objects more by shaking them, banging them, turning them around and chewing on them. This is the way that all babies seem to learn about the relationship between cause and effect. An *action* (such as the shaking of a rattle) produces a *result* (such as a noise).

Dexterity will increase so rapidly from the third month to the sixth month that soon your child can not only reach out, grasp and release, but can manipulate the toy with considerable accuracy.

What a wonderful discovery hands and fingers are! Babies find that they can do so many different things. They hold Mom's or Dad's fingers, hold brightly colored toys, touch all kinds of interesting surfaces that are smooth, hard, rough, soft. And, best of all, you can suck on them! What sensations!

Further experiments prove that these objects are different from the parents' fingers, blankets or toys. When he bites the end of a wooden rattle, he feels something hard. When he jabs his thumb into his mouth, he receives a very different feeling. After he mouths the rattle and, then, his thumb again and again, he suddenly becomes aware that his thumb is soft while his rattle is hard. At some point, when he is sucking his thumb there is a breakthrough. The discovery: this toy (the thumb) is ME! This toy (the rattle) is *something else!*

Once the baby becomes aware that he exists apart from the objects around him, the learning process accelerates. Now he can concentrate on what is going on around him instead of putting all his efforts into gaining body control. Baby experiences what Dr. Arnold Gesell refers to as "touch hunger"—he must touch everything in sight.

Now that your baby is making more purposeful hand and arm movements, and is generally more active, you will need to move the fluttering, delicate mobiles out of reach. You may want to hang them from the ceiling or in front of a window to catch the breeze. Your baby's area of focus is considerably expanded now, and he is taking in more distant visual impressions more clearly.

RATTLES

The classic toy for a baby who is learning to touch, reach and grasp is the rattle. This ancient, universal object is probably the oldest of toys. From the crude gourd used by primitive people to the elaborate silver and gold versions made for princes, the rattle has proven to be the perfect plaything to soothe and amuse an infant.

Rattles have been intricately adorned with gold and silver bells and tassels. They have been made of rubber, bone, ivory, china and wood. Rattles, once religious objects, were used to announce the arrival of the gods. The medieval jester waved his rattle decked with streamers and bells at court; Eskimos used rattles to entice seals from the water; portraits of Renaissance children show them holding ivory rattles to protect them from the evil eye.

Quite an impressive history for such a simple toy! Your baby, quite oblivious to these facts, is likely to think of his rattle as nothing more than noisy food. But, don't overlook the value of this deceptively simple toy. The rattle doesn't give away the secret that it is actually the precursor to all the more complex tools that will be used later in life.

Now the rattle may be thrust into your baby's hand as a pacifier. Its function, however, is more than passive. Instead, the rattle is helping your baby develop the basic skills of coordinating eye and hand movements. The ability to hold a spoon or a pencil and, eventually, to eat or write begins in the cradle with the baby exploring a simple rattle. Hands that he can pull apart and put together, that can pick up and throw a ball, screw a cap, tie a shoe or play the piano, depend on the practice in eye-hand coordination that starts in early childhood.

Rattles come in a multitude of shapes, sizes, materials and designs—everything from the expensive silver dumbbell to the plastic ring and ball. There are balls, clowns and animals with noise makers inside. Some have teething rings or edges. Your baby won't be teething for another month or two, but these toys will go into his mouth. The most important thing for baby is that the rattle be pleasant to look at, hold and listen to.

Many rattles produce pleasant, interesting noises. Try for a variety of shapes and sounds in forms that invite different hand positions. Your baby will appreciate a range of tactile sensations. If he still cannot easily release his grip, replace the rattle he is clutching with another design.

There are many innovations on the basic design. Here is a collection of rattles which will offer your baby pure delight and new learning experiences:

• JOHNSON & JOHNSON's *Spinner Rattle* provides several stimulating elements needed in baby's first hand-held toy. Every shake of the Spinner Rattle produces a movement, a sound and color that will delight his curiosity. The contemporary dumbbell-shaped rattle has a clear area on one end of a yellow and red striped center. A teething ring is attached to the other end. The spinner and red beads within the clear casing provide exciting visual stimulation for the infant.

(Note: All Johnson & Johnson toys come with a teaching guide. Each guide details the benefits of the toy and suggests play activities for the child and parental involvement.)

• JOHNSON & JOHNSON's *Tracking Tube* is also dumbbell-shaped. A bright red ball glides through a clear liquid center tube and disappears into the yellow ball at either end of the tube. Suddenly, the red ball reappears when the tube is tilted. Each end is soft for squeezing. Squeak and jingle sounds are produced as a result of baby's efforts. The Tracking Tube helps to develop eye coordination and tracking skills in the newborn.

• JOHNSON & JOHNSON's *Wiggle Worm* is a long colorful and easy-to-grasp soft toy with a variety of manipulative experiences. Baby can tug at and hold onto the three blue rings jutting from the back of the worm. Once he has a grip on them he will promptly chew on one of the rings to see what it's all about. As he hugs this soft wiggly creature, he discovers that it can produce several interesting sounds—the head squeaks, the body rattles, the tail crackles in response to baby's pokes and squeezes.

SPINNER RATTLE
Johnson & Johnson

• JOHNSON & JOHNSON's *Red Rings* is a teether and bell-ring rattle. From above it looks like a fried egg with a blue ball for a yolk surrounded by two red rings. Red Rings stimulates the visual and motor skills baby is developing now as he pulls and twists the flexible rings. This toy is made of a special plastic so that it is tough enough to resist baby's pulling and tugging, yet soft enough for teething. The three rings wobble as the rattle is turned over and over.

• FISHER-PRICE has a collection of colorful animal-shaped plastic rattles. They are easy to hold and flourish. One favorite is a happy-faced Sunflower Rattle with eyes that move about on one side of the rattle; there is a mirror so babies can see their own smiling faces on the other side.

• CHILD GUIDANCE's *Peek-A-Boo Rattle* is similar in concept. Baby can spin the durable plastic ball and produce a smiling face. These rattles, in pastel colors, are also easy to grasp.

There are several imported rattles that offer baby familiar yet interesting interpretations of the basic shapes:

• KIDDICRAFT's *Teddy Bear Rattle* contains three brightly colored beads which rattle against a light refracting material. The baby experiences movement, noise and light as he shakes his teddy. On the reverse side is an unbreakable mirror. Kiddicraft's Ring Rattle (six colored beads which roll around a clear plastic and sonically-welded ring) is lightweight and easy to hold when your baby first learns how to grasp.

• BERCHET makes one of the most delightful rattles we have seen. This rattle, in the shape of a bright yellow tree, contains colored beads which roll around the inside of the branches. The trunk is the rattle's handle.

• AMBI has created a most unusual looking rattle. Two grinning yellow faces in the shape of gears are permanently meshed. As the baby moves one face, the other face circles around it. Ambi's *Shiny Rattles* come in three graceful shapes—a red fish, a yellow snail, a white goose. Each rattle has an unbreakable convex mirror on both sides and is filled with three colored beads to shake and rattle around. Most attractive!

• PLAYSKOOL has designed two whimsical creatures—a Butterfly and a Honeybee. Each *Happy Rattle* has a transparent wing section so that your baby can watch the multi-colored beads roll around inside.

• TOYS TO GROW ON's catalog offers a collection of classic wooden infant toys. The five-piece set gives your baby a variety of shapes and sizes to hold and explore. Each shape, in smooth natural wood, makes a different type of ring or clack sound.

HAPPY RATTLES
Playskool

• FISHER-PRICE and PLAYSKOOL make the popular new soft rattles. The rattles' basic shapes are soft, cuddly clowns, bunnies and birds in a washable patterned fabric. The rattling sound comes from the head or face of the toy. These are easy to manipulate and fun to hold and love. *Soft Shakes* are by Fisher-Price and *Soft Tuggies* are made by Playskool.

• CHILD GUIDANCE offers two favorite, familiar characters in the soft doll and rattle category. Sesame Street's *Huggable Big Bird* and *Huggable Cookie Monster* are very appealing, cuddly pals that rattle as baby plays.

• BRIO's beautifully painted wooden rattles in traditional shapes —bell, stacking rattle, dumbbell—will be great toys for baby as his grip strengthens.

• JOHNSON & JOHNSON's *Rolling Circus* combines a rattle with a puzzle and action toy. Spheres, circles and stars move about in a clear dumbbell shape. A yellow and red star on the outside of the rattle slides and flip-flops as the baby rotates the toy. This action helps to develop hand and finger coordination and the Circus is suggested for parent and child rolling games.

Now baby begins to play for longer periods of time—up to three-fourths of an hour. He is exploring with his hands as well as following patterns and lights and colors with his eyes. He associates the sound of the rattle with his movements. He discovers that he has caused these sounds to happen.

Now that your baby has mastered the art of holding and waving a rattle, he is ready for more active play. Toys are needed which will give your child a chance to practice his reach, grasp and release.

ROLLING CIRCUS
Johnson & Johnson

CRIB GYMS

A Crib Gym is the basic toy for the baby who is ready to use his hands. Crib Gyms foster grasping and reaching. They help to stimulate eye-hand coordination and help baby realize his own movements have caused the motion and the noise. Crib Gyms should be placed within the baby's comfortable reach so he can create his own visual, aural and tactile stimulation. Baby's not just playing—he is learning about cause and effect.

Safety note: Before you hang the Crib Gym, check it carefully. If the suspension straps are equipped with metal springs, test the springs to see that the baby cannot pinch his fingers in them.

These gyms not only provide hand exercises, they also help an infant realize that despite his small size, he can still do things to affect his environment. He becomes so intrigued with his ability to bat things and cause movement that he keeps practicing these much-needed hand skills. Gradually his eyes and hands begin to work together better; his aim improves, and he develops his eye-hand coordination.

Once the Crib Gym, with its brightly colored objects dangling in baby's line of vision, is placed across the crib, a number of impulses are set in motion. The baby gazes at the tempting cluster and then swipes out at it. He may miss on the first try. But he is determined to investigate these intriguing shapes. He raises his arm and lunges out toward the gym. Something moves; something makes a pleasant noise; something bounces. Success! The pattern begins again, this time more vigorously.

A baby reaches out for an object with both arms at three months. He starts with his arms at his sides and brings them up in front of his body. At this time he may make contact with closed fists. Now he is beginning to remember what he has just tried to do, so that a second attempt may get better results. As he becomes more and more aware of self, he senses that his hands and feet are extensions of him and that he can make an unlimited number of things happen with them.

You will notice that the Crib Gym will provide a variety of activities for the baby. He will work on it with both his hands and feet. As he becomes familiar with each shape and pull toy, he will begin using the gym as a piece of gymnastic equipment. Soon he will grab it and pull his body off the mattress. Eventually, he will do tricks with two hands at the same time. While he is holding onto one object, he will manipulate another shape on the rod. This seemingly random action involves the sort of coordination that is the basis for all fine-motor skills the baby will be developing in years to come.

There are many interesting Crib Gyms on the market designed to excite and develop baby's evolving skills. Some come with rattles, plastic balls and bells, flowers, and music boxes that play when your baby pulls a cord.

You can make your own crib gym from your own materials. Secure a bar across the top of the crib and hang objects from it on wide, strong lengths of elastic. Some of the graspable things might be teethers, rattles, a ball or rubber block inside a mesh bag, large thread spools, an older child's wooden beads—securely strung, or even a stuffed animal. His first instinct will be to bring all objects to his mouth, so you will want to make sure all parts are securely attached and that there is nothing that can choke him or that he can swallow. Your baby will enjoy these contrivances enormously. He will push and swing these dangling objects, grab them, handle them and suck on them.

There are many colorful and exciting Crib Gyms that will totally absorb your baby. Among the most useful and attractive are:

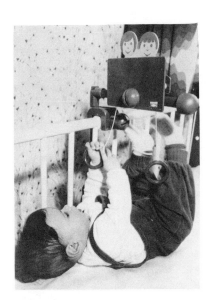

CRIB GYM SYSTEM
Fischerform

• FISCHERFORM's well-thought-out crib gym. It has been designed to take advantage of the baby's growing abilities. A main rod can be attached to the crib railings. A number of carefully graded learning toys can be hung on the basic crib mount. Packaged with clear designations of age, these toys can be selected to match the baby's developing abilities to reach out, to grasp, to push and pull. For instance, the Fun Focus Mirror aids in the development of eye coordination and self-recognition. Swing Blocks are added as baby begins to grasp; Spin Flower, a Music Box and Mini Trapeze would be added to the bar as baby grows and is able to handle several activities. The toys come in bright primary colors.

• JOHNSON & JOHNSON's very friendly looking *Piglet Crib Gym*. This soft gym is easy to attach to the crib. Three cloth-covered piglets respond to your baby's pokes and tugs with a squeak, a rattle or a crackle. The piglets are filled with safe and machine washable materials. The piglets can be removed and used as lovable companions when baby gets older and is sitting up.

• BERCHET's *Crib Activity Center* which presents basic shapes in an unusual way. The main rod is divided into four colorful sections. The items that hang from the sections are a small bell with a yellow ball; a dark-blue stylized fish with a ball tummy; a bright-red chick to swing back and forth; a yellow ring to pull.

• FISHER-PRICE's *Play Gym* is a departure from the usual ring and bar shapes. Dangling from the crossbar are a flower and a butterfly for pushing and turning around; a clown to squeeze; and a large see-through barrel which revolves around the center bar.

• BRIO's classic *Cradle Gym*, beautifully painted in vivid primary colors, features polished wooden cylinders and beads hung from a crossbar.

• KIDDICRAFT's striking Gym with plastic pulls and batting balls that make noise when manipulated.

• TOYS TO GROW ON's two Crib Gyms with different shapes to look at and textures to feel. The first is a very pleasing wooden chime. Four smiling Crib Friends look at your baby, inviting him to touch. Each figure makes a tingling ring when tapped.

The other is a soft shapes gym featuring a squeaking star, rattling ball, jingling drum and a ring strung on a soft cord. Each item can be removed and played with individually when baby is older.

Crib Gyms are best used when your child is between three and six months. This is the time when baby is still on his back a great deal of the time and will look forward to the kind of stimulation that a Crib Gym affords. As soon as he can sit up by himself and becomes more active, your baby will need items and toys that meet more advanced needs.

Between three and six months, your growing baby will gain considerably more control over his body movements. Early in this period your child will hold his head steady and be able to sit with support, and some babies at six months will be sitting alone. In any case, he will be fingering, touching, holding and experimenting with the feel, texture and shape of everything.

PULL TOYS

A variation on the Crib Gym which illustrates the important concept of *cause* and *effect* is the pull toy. These toys attach to the side of the crib and are based on the jack-in-the-box concept. The baby pulls a ring at the bottom of the pull; and music plays, a hand moves and objects move about. He is not only excited by the motion he has caused, but he has made something wonderful happen. *HE* is the instigator of the action and sound.

• CHILD GUIDANCE's delightful *Peek-A-Boo Clown*. Pull on the Clown's bow tie and his large hands cover his eyes. Release the tie and his hands open. The soft nose squeaks when squeezed; the flower on his hat spins and his eyes wink at baby. Your baby has found a friend who performs in marvelous ways when he tells him to.

• PLAYSKOOL's *Lullabye Bird* with its sunny yellow bird playing a guitar. When baby rocks the bird, it plays one of ten popular nursery songs. Or, it can be set to play for 20 continuous minutes to lull baby to sleep.

• TOMY's *Busy Bungalow* featuring a charming musical house that plays "Mary Had A Little Lamb" when the knob is turned.

• FISHER-PRICE's *Funflower* which is a lovely, pokeable toy. Six brightly colored cloth petals frame a smiling face which squeaks when touched.

• PLAYSKOOL's *Sweet Sounds* with its charming version of a touch flower, which also attaches to the side of the crib. Baby can make three different sounds—a squeak, a rattle, a jingle, when he squeezes the Touch Flower.

FUNFLOWER
Fisher-Price Toys

At about five months you may notice a sudden change in your child's response to the people that come and go in your home. He may cry at a strange face and become selective about whom he allows to hold and carry him. He has finally recognized *you* and his other close and dear friends. He now knows when the person approaching him is not someone he sees every day.

Now that he recognizes people, he will encounter one of his first serious social problems—separation from you. A baby under nine months is not aware that a person or an object has an independent

CANTON   MADISON COUNTY
PUBLIC LIBRARY SYSTEM

existence. The peek-a-boo game offers him a way of working out this problem and will fascinate him for months and even years to come. At first, baby may be a little put off when your hands obscure your face, but your reappearance and your "boo!" will reassure him. He is learning about *disappearance and reappearance*—that out of sight is not out of the world. He is beginning to realize that you may not always be there, but you will come back.

Now is the time to play with the peek-a-boo toys mentioned earlier. Show your baby the rattle or doll or Clown pull gym. Talk to him about the smiling face, the colors. As you and your child play and as the faces disappear and reappear, baby positively responds to the activity around him. These "people" go away but Mom or Dad don't, nor does he. In fact, baby can control when they go away and when they come back. These simple games played with the parents help to increase the feeling of trust that your baby needs to develop for emotional well-being.

Infant researchers claim that many parents do not realize how important it is to play regularly with their babies. The essentials—feeding, bathing and changing—are not enough. Sharing games together is a must.

Dr. Alvin N. Eden writes in his book, *Positive Parenting*, "Infants are very attuned to their surroundings. Emotional stability is nurtured by friendly, familiar, affectionate voices, laughter and singing. Babies also require and respond to close physical contact. There is no such thing as too much touching, holding and carrying around."

Bath time may be the highlight of his day, and he will laugh and play avidly with bath toys. He will even begin to vocalize more seriously and will carry on little conversations with himself and with you. From the start, talk simply but coherently to your child. Try to avoid baby talk—that's not what he's striving to learn. When you speak to him pronounce words the way you want him to say them so he will hear the correct sounds from the beginning.

Your baby's legs and feet will not actually be the focal point of his development yet, but he is using them vigorously and beginning to be aware of their existence. He will notice his toes, play with them and even manage to put them in his mouth! You will want to provide exercise for those active, kicking legs and feet long before he begins to stand and walk. Think about a kicking toy.

A kicking toy is essentially a variation of the cradle gym. As a matter of fact, your baby will kick at his gym and sometimes catch his foot in the rings. You can make a very satisfactory kicking toy at home. Select a big, soft cuddle toy that makes a noise when kicked and attach it to an elastic band tied across the crib from one side to the other. Make sure that the toy is placed over your child's legs so that he can reach it with his feet.

As your baby approaches six months, a baby bouncer suspended from a door jamb will provide excellent exercise for his legs and feet; and he will need a minimum of supervision. Among the most available models are the Baby Bouncer, the Baby Jumper Swing and the Jolly Jumper. All operate on the same principle: the baby is put into the seat or padded saddle which is suspended from a ring or bar so that his feet just touch the floor. His instinct is to push against the floor with his feet, causing the swing to bounce. Babies love these bouncers. They also love to sit in bouncing chairs or walkers. Exercise the same caution you did with the crib gyms and be certain that your baby's fingers cannot be caught in the springs.

These very nearly indispensable bouncers should not be confused with swings in which the baby merely sits passively while a motor or a push from Mother provides the movement. The jumping-bouncing swings require the baby to do the work in order to enjoy the fun. He not only gets valuable pre-walking exercise, but also learns that his own actions can bring pleasure.

As he gains control of his body, he will be a handful, and you will have to keep an eye on him all the time. One glance away, and he will wriggle right off his bath table and bounce across the floor before you know it! He will need a safe, secure place to play, so this is the time to invest in a good, sturdy playpen. Most child development experts feel that the playpen is a great help to a busy mother. But care should be taken that it not become a convenient device for her and a prison for the baby. Certainly a baby of six months and over needs ample opportunity to be out on the floor, free to experiment with his wiggling and pivoting—both precursors to crawling.

As your baby approaches six months, much of his waking day may be spent in his playpen. He does not yet understand the difference between *in* and *out* and he has not yet begun to crawl. He will enjoy lying on his stomach, rolling over and sitting, examining the things around him. He should have a supply of objects to examine, test and exercise his command over. He will be consumed with transferring things from one hand to the other, fingering, mouthing, touching everything in reach. He has perfected his release and will delight in exercising this new skill at every opportunity by dropping and pitching toys.

The baby of nearly six months is a much more social individual than he was just a short time ago. He will begin to want to play with you rather than just by himself. If you hold him up to a mirror he will be truly excited at discovering you and him in the mirror. He will pat the mirror and talk to it, cooing and gurgling and thoroughly enjoying himself. Your baby will begin to learn language during this three month period. When parents talk to the child and respond to the baby's verbal play, this language learning process is stimulated, and baby wants to do more, learn more, say more.

BABY MIRRORS

Encourage the baby to imitate your simple movements and sounds. Hold him up to a mirror and let him see for himself. A mirror is so pleasing to a baby that he will even stop crying to look and smile at himself. As he reaches out to touch the "someone" in the mirror, he is continuing to discover that other people exist outside himself. He would revel in having his very own little mirror to make faces at and communicate with. It should be free of flaws and distortions to avoid disorienting his visual perception; and it should be large enough for the baby to see his entire face clearly. Your baby's mirror should be made of polished metal rather than glass and encased in a plastic, rubber or smooth-edged wooden frame. In order for the baby to see himself clearly, the mirror should be about six inches from his eyes. These baby mirrors come both in inexpensive dime store models as well as the more costly imported versions.

Many of the Crib Gyms and rattles feature a mirror as part of the toy so that baby can compare his face with the face on the toy.

• KIDDICRAFT makes *See Me TV*, a mirror in a very familiar shape—a TV set. The mirror is set in a bright-orange frame with clicking knobs to turn and even a place for the insertion of a family photo. The Teddy Bear Rattle baby has been playing with also contains an unbreakable mirror on one side. There also is a large Play Mirror set in a frame with six finger holes placed so that baby can grasp and hold easily. The mirror has been described as the "ultimate discovery toy."

• FISCHERFORM's *Crawly Mirror* is a unique toy. The weighted mirror is set on large yellow wheels which move slowly yet gently, while keeping the mirror at a proper angle for viewing by your baby.

• PLAYSKOOL has designed *Play Mirror* in the shape of a drum with large knobs around the mirror that baby can grab. This toy is safe for teething and also entertains with a rattling sound. *Baby Mirror Ring Rattle* is another mirror and teether/rattle combination that can be fastened to the crib, playpen or even to baby's clothes. It comes in pretty pastel colors with animal shapes framing the mirror.

There are some marvelous games you can play with the baby's mirror which will provide new visual experiences. Capture a ray of sunshine through an open window (or a beam of light from a lamp) and move its reflection around the walls and ceiling for your baby to follow with his eyes. Of course you should be careful not to shine the light in his sensitive eyes. Or, with your baby sitting on your lap, hold the mirror in front of him so it reflects a favorite toy that is behind him. He may not catch on at first, but it will be an exciting moment for both of you when he realizes what reflections are all about, and he turns around to find the actual toy!

DOLLS

As he relates more and more to the world around him, his dolls and animals will play an increasingly important role in your baby's life. He might, like Linus in "Peanuts," become attached totally to a raggedy old blanket. Be sure to provide him with soft, cuddly friends to hold and fondle. Security crib toys will still be important, and you can add to them as your pocketbook allows. Baby can now be comforted and snuggled into bed with the whole Peanuts gang on sheets, towels and blankets, available in department stores. Snoopy himself comes in all shapes and sizes as do other story book favorites—Winnie-the-Pooh, the Sesame Street characters, Raggedy Ann and Andy. These dolls and animals, soft and cuddly, serve as transitional objects to help baby accept the change from one person or situation to another.

They represent the human figure caring for him, and give him a chance to express love and affection whether it be a hug or a quick fling over the side of the crib.

A truly beautiful doll collection from COROLLE is brought to life by French designer Catherine Refabert. She has created very soft, delicate "tender dolls" intended to "stimulate affection, fondness, attachment, love and warmth" in the child who holds one. A very important design feature of all Corolle dolls for any age group is that each one is sized to fit the child's hand, is scaled to the child's body as well as proportioned to the weight of the child. Therefore they are the perfect size to hold comfortably. The Babi Corolle selection includes pastel animal and baby doll figures.

Baby's first Teddy can be found in the best stuffed animal store in the world, F.A.O. Schwarz. Besides the traditional brown teddy bear, they feature a pink and blue teddy from Trupa of Italy. Schwarz also has a soft fleece lamb that is very appealing. This gentle, sweet friend is also by Trupa.

There are many practical and appealing dolls on the market:

• KATHE KRUSE has a lovely collection of terry cloth dolls that come in seven colors and are made in one piece so that baby can't chew them apart. The duck, bear, horse or doll never lose their shape, are non-toxic and float in water, so they are perfect for bath time play as well.

• FISHER-PRICE's first dolls come in a variety of shapes. *Lolly*, a pink-faced charmer dressed in pink gingham, is a wonderful first friend for your baby. The *Animal Grabbers* (a selection of cute animal faces) that include the pink Pig, blue Elephant and yellow Puppy can be grabbed by their floppy ears which are very chewable.

• The FISHER-PRICE *Peek-A-Boo Baby* is one that Mom, Dad and baby can play with together. Baby is snuggly wrapped in his blanket. Open the blanket and Peek-A-Boo baby's arms reach out to greet you.

Vegetables may play a surprising role in your baby's life, and we recommend *Vegimals* by FREEMOUNTAIN TOYS of Vermont. This is a collection of machine-washable, plush-fabric vegetables. Who can really resist a smiling broccoli?

Again, all stuffed animals and dolls should be carefully checked for any removable parts, such as button eyes, whistles or any sharp pieces. Test them yourself. If you can remove anything, your baby can, too.

Another reminder: toys should be made of non-allergenic, long-lasting and, preferably, washable materials. If your child becomes attached to a toy, it will get a lot of hard wear and tear.

As he approaches six months your baby has learned to focus his eyes well; he has gained command of his head, arms and hands; and he is beginning to sit up by himself. Eye-hand coordination has been developed to the degree that he can reach for a specific object, grasp it and release it. The almost-six-month-old can use his fingers separately, although not very surely. He is rapidly becoming a person in his own right and taking much more interest in the family and life around him. What a long way he has come in six short months!

These have been relatively calm months, because he can't yet move about on his own and is easily protected in his crib, carriage or playpen. Enjoy this period of relative tranquility, for, much to his delight, he will soon be on the move. Give him the things he needs to see, touch and handle, and enjoy your happy, contented baby as he awakens every day to the excitement of his expanding world and his growing mastery of it.

Toys are to children what books and records are to grown-ups. Dolls, rattles, activity toys are all mentally and physically stimulating. These new friends help your baby learn about spatial relationships, color, texture and sound. Most importantly, they help him learn about himself.

As your baby rapidly changes in the next few months from the infant in a crib to a baby on-the-move, dashing and darting about, everything speeds up. One day he *cannot* reach the items he is swiping at or turn a knob on his Crib Gym. But, lo and behold, the very next day he *can!*

LOLLY DOLL
Fisher-Price Toys

VEGIMALS
Freemountain Toys

Six to Nine Months
In and Out of Everything

Can you believe it? Your baby is now six months old! This is the halfway point in this very important first year during which your child will grow faster and, actually, learn more than at any other time in his entire life.

As you have probably observed by now, your baby's physical development has progressed from the top down: first he gained control over his eyes, then his head, then his hands and arms, then his back. At this mid-point between birth and a year, he is still quite sedentary, but he is becoming increasingly skillful with his hands—grasping, transferring and manipulating objects. As this next three month period begins, your baby gains command of his trunk so that he can sit without support, and, later, will begin to crawl and creep. (The difference is that in crawling the baby's stomach never gets off the floor, but creeping is accomplished on hands and knees or hands and feet, with the stomach well raised from the floor.)

At six months the infant is becoming a child as he turns actively toward the outside world. Your child can become so active at this stage that he hardly stops to look and listen. According to Dr. T. Berry Brazelton, "The human infant is surely endowed with the ability to take in, to store and to learn important things from his environment from birth. There are three forces that propel an infant from one stage of development to the next: an instinctual drive to survive, no matter how complex the world may seem; a drive toward mastery of himself and his world, which can best be seen in the excitement he expresses as he makes each developmental step; and finally, the drive to fit into, to identify with and to become part of his environment."

The first two drives come from within the infant, claims Dr. Brazelton. The third comes from the environment and this nurtures the others. "If the environment is sterile or non-responsive, the other drives will either come to a standstill or wither away."

Practically all of your child's waking time will now be spent out of the crib and much of it out of the playpen as well, so he will be ready for new learning playthings. He may still enjoy the crib gym for short periods upon awakening, but would probably like the challenge of a more complicated toy.

Proper stimulation is as important as fulfilling the basic needs of the baby. As he adds to his abilities day by day at a very rapid rate of growth, take time to observe what he is capable of doing. Now, the playthings should increase in number and variety. But, be careful not to over-stimulate the baby—for that can be as much of a turn-off as not enough stimulation.

It is going to be tempting to dump numerous toys into the crib or playpen and the baby is apt to be bombarded from all angles with too many dangling, moving, musical, twirling objects. Each toy introduced at this time will provide baby with a combination of interesting things to do and will offer a number of challenges. So don't overwhelm him.

Examine each toy before giving it to the baby. And, then give him time to study the toy and to examine it. Talk to him about the toy and its parts. Help him get started.

However, now is also the time to allow the child to experiment with a variety of situations so that he can experience the satisfaction of "managing" by himself. At this stage, he is ready to shift his interest from human beings to inanimate objects. As he does, his whole world opens up and begins to widen.

There are two main developmental tasks the baby must handle during this period:
- He must learn how to discriminate.
- He must learn how to control his own body, how to be active.

Your child is learning how to master the world around by moving toward the objects he wants and grasping them. Babies are better able to differentiate among the objects they see around them, and, slowly, they begin to recognize their uses.

His body control is much improved as he first learns how to sit and then stand by himself. The hand now really takes on its grasping function, Your baby grabs at anything within reach. So, it is important for children during this time to have things to hold and play with.

Your baby will begin to select and separate his favorite toy from the others and, as he becomes more active and somewhat independent, he will begin to remove toys that *don't* please him. You can tell that he is positively interested in amusing himself.

In addition, the baby is developing memory, and now he can experiment with the function of an item—play with it, turn away, come back and continue the interrupted activity.

At about eight months, the baby begins to realize that a covered object has not just disappeared—it is still there, under the blanket, even if he can't see it. Babies now like to imitate. They will copy your movements such as knocking, waving, nodding or clapping. They imitate sounds, repeating what is said to them. They may not retain words for long, but all of this babbling and gooing and ma-ma-ing is the start of language development.

These three months are referred to as the early exploratory stage. Your child is rapidly developing many of the skills that make it possible to explore and interact with the world around him. He will now reach for objects and successfully grab them, even tiny ones. The baby now has excellent control of his hand and is fascinated with manipulating the various objects he can see and grab. His eyes and ears function very effectively. He can focus well on objects near and far and can locate sounds without difficulty. He has excellent head control. He will be spending more and more time in the sitting position so that he can see more of what is going on around him. Babies now learn how to crawl and, then, cruise along holding onto furniture. Now, he's got the mobility to investigate what is happening some distance away.

His interest in games increases every day. One favorite pastime is to drop toys and objects from a height—say, a highchair, and watch to see what happens. "Thud!" "Splat!" "Jingle!" He is not trying to drive you crazy. But he will continue to drop everything he can get his hands on over and over again until he finally masters the function and remembers what he has accomplished. Curiosity is growing. He will want to touch and taste everything he can find and hold.

It is essential that you encourage him in every way you can. Give him the opportunity to expand his skills and horizons.

Dr. Arnold Gesell calls this period "a heyday for manipulation." The baby's hands are becoming increasingly well coordinated, and even after he learns to creep there will be quiet periods when he will want to work with his hands. You will observe this sequence: he will concentrate on an object he is holding, then, suddenly spy another object and reach for it with his other hand. He will then put one thing down, and transfer the remaining object from one hand to the other—all the while carefully studying the shape, size and weight of everything he holds. He rotates his wrist so he can examine things from all sides. He has such a compelling urge to use his hands to feel and explore things that he will even be content to play by himself for short periods of time. At about eight months, he will acquire the ability to use his thumb and forefinger with a pincer movement, an ability which distinguishes human beings from the rest of the animal kingdom.

ACTIVITY CENTERS

Activity Centers with their numerous components of knobs, cranks, dials, doors which move and make sounds will give your baby early experiences in cause and effect.

• FISHER-PRICE's *Activity Center* has ten fun things for your child to do. For instance, he can look in a mirror, call home on a telephone dial, spin a knob, ring a bell and push a rabbit along after a turtle. Their *Turn & Learn Activity Center* is a pyramid-shaped toy that can be carried around. Each side features another type of finger/hand manipulation.

• AMBI's *Fun House* is another activity board that is filled with fun things to do that will stimulate your baby's skills. A door opens, a dog barks, the clown pops up and waves at your child. Baby can twirl, slide figures, twist and fit objects into others. He can play peek-a-boo with himself when he discovers the mirror behind the blue door. The Fun House is painted in bright, primary colors and attaches to crib, playpen or can be propped up on the floor.

• BRIO makes a playboard with a bright yellow background on which is painted a light blue bunny holding an inviting green ball to pull. The red flower contains a mirror in the center; the tree grows red "apples" that baby cannot wait to pull off.

• CHILD GUIDANCE's *The Busy Box* is now a tradition in most families. The original Busy Box has entertained millions of babies since its introduction. This activity board helps to feed your baby's interest in operating simple gadgets. This entertainment center combines ten activities that babies love to try and that are great for cause and effect. Pull open the door and see yourself in the mirror; turn the dial and hear a bell ring; spin the knob and watch a multitude of colors twirl around.

Another variation on the busy box theme is Child Guidance's Sesame Street *Take-Along Busy House*. This brightly colored yellow house offers baby five activities to test motor skills. Push the button and the green door opens to reveal the Cookie Monster munching on a handful of cookies. Baby can play peek-a-boo with Ernie by raising and lowering the window ledge. There is also a ball to squeeze, a mirror to peer into and a pole to spin. Busy House is easy to carry

**SESAME STREET
TAKE-ALONG BUSY HOUSE**
Child Guidance

about by its Sesame Street sign that serves as a handle. Child Guidance's *Busy Choo-Choo* is a delightful first activities toy that can be used
as a pull toy when baby gets older. Seven activities hold baby's attention: the train makes all the appropriate sounds and has a multi-colored
wheel to twirl and three colored beads to slide; a telephone dial and
tumble bead cowcatcher add to the fun of playing with this Busy
Choo-Choo. Its imaginative design makes this an activity toy your
child will enjoy using as a push-and-pull toy in the next few months.

DISNEY MUSICAL BUSY BOX
Child Guidance

Child Guidance also has an electronic musical *Busy Box*. Eight
nursery tunes reward your baby's push and pull activities. Each play
feature produces a soft melody. After play, the music box shuts off
automatically. Walt Disney characters are featured on the Child Guidance Busy Box.

At this stage, nature has given your baby a tremendous hunger
to examine, handle, mouth and manipulate everything he encounters.
This is a time of discovering the outside world. Your baby needs a
variety of simple manipulative toys amd all sorts of other objects to
give him the rich sensorial input and stimulation that he is searching
for. Fortunately, many of the most satisfactory items are common
household objects: nested measuring cups, measuring spoons, wooden
spoons, clothespins (the old-fashioned wooden ones, not the kind with
springs), plastic freezer containers, cupcake pans and other small baking pans, empty Band-Aid cans, boxes, etc.

Good items to buy are lightweight plastic blocks, tissue paper to
crumple and tear, a squeaky squeeze toy, a musical rattle or a bell with
a handle, a basket or box for putting in and taking out other toys.

Your baby can now open his fist and let go of objects at will. Soon
he will learn to throw on purpose. You may think he is being perverse
when he drops a toy from the playpen or feeding table five hundred
times and each time cries for you to get it for him, and then immediately proceeds to drop or throw it again. Not at all—he is merely
practicing his new skill and is unwittingly going through a pre-
counting exercise.

You can save your back by using short strings or shoelaces to tie
toys to his playpen or bounce chair. He won't be able to hoist them
back up himself right away, but they'll be a lot easier for you to
retrieve. Good items for tying are a teether, a metal cup with handle,
empty adhesive tape reels and things to bang like a pot cover and a
wooden spoon. There is even a plastic feeding spoon that can be
attached to the high chair by a plastic cord tied to a suction cup. When
your baby throws the spoon, it won't even hit the floor but will just
hang there until you pull it up.

SHAPE SORTER
Fisher-Price Toys

BALLS IN A BOWL
Johnson & Johnson

DROP AND RETRIEVE TOYS

Here are two toys that are designed to satisfy your baby's need to drop and retrieve:

• FISHER-PRICE's *Shape Sorter* has four different shapes for your baby to sort out and match and drop and, then, retrieve. Baby has to match the shape with the right opening and drop it through. When he opens the door marked with the symbol of the shape, the item returns. A smiling face on the top of the box gives encouragement. Begin together by showing your baby where each shape goes. Have him imitate your actions. Talk about the colors. Play peek-a-boo as you let him discover just where the green triangle went. This toy combines elements that challenge several skills that baby is just acquiring. He is learning how to discriminate shape and color; he is experimenting with *in* and *out*; and he is making discoveries about dropping objects.

• JOHNSON & JOHNSON's *Balls in a Bowl* is a unique filling and dumping toy. A large yellow ball is a container for three smaller balls which contain brightly colored spinners that rotate, rattle or twirl. This bright and lively combination teaches the child concepts like big and small; inside and outside. Balls in a Bowl can be used in the bath.

Banging is an important activity when rattles have lost their charm and the baby's hands are reaching out for something new. Let your child bang on plastic ice cream containers or empty coffee cans with plastic lids over both ends. These will produce a good dull sound. Offer him a variety of materials so that he can create a variety of different sounds. He can bang a metal spoon on a pie tin, clash two pot covers like cymbals or clap two wooden blocks together. There are small Indian drums with soft tops that he can beat with his hand.

Pushing, throwing and rolling things around also greatly amuse your child. Roly-poly toys with weighted bottoms that roll back up after being pushed over allow him to experience an intriguing manipulative maneuver. A very practical, two-handled training cup by FIRST YEARS rights itself even if the baby doesn't put it down correctly. Since the cup is self-righting because of its shape and it does not have a weighted bottom, it is easier for small hands to pick up and handle.

• FIRST YEARS makes several musical roly-poly toys in clown and bear shapes.

• KIDDICRAFT's collection of roly-poly toys is one of the best on the market for design and types of figures available:

Wobbly Colors is perfect as your baby's first fitting and color sorting toy. Four squares in vivid red, blue, yellow and green each hold a ball in the matching color. The ball is weighted to wobble when rolled by the child.

Watermate Duck contains a small yellow duck sitting on a pebbled pond. He remains upright, however baby rolls the clear ball.

Rocking Bear Rattle is a friendly figure which loves to be rocked back and forth.

Doggy Dumbbell completes the group. A playful red puppy with soulful moving eyes rattles when baby plays with him. The curved base of the toy allows the child to rock the puppy back and forth on a flat surface.

• CHICCO, from Italy, has designed a series of more grown-up looking roly-poly toys—the ship's captain, clown and soccer player all make music when pushed.

• AMBI's *Jack-In-The-Ball* combines two well-known toys into one—a roly-poly and a Jack-in-the-box. When baby pushes on the ball, a clown pops up making a squeaking sound. Push the clown down and the toy becomes a ball again.

• FISHER-PRICE's *Chime Ball* contains a storybook land within a clear globe. As the ball moves around in response to baby's push, the hobby horse and swans rock to the music of the chimes.

• FISHER-PRICE's *Three Men in a Tub* is a roly-poly toy which also floats. The butcher dressed in bright yellow, the baker in his white chef's hat and the candlestick maker all ready for bedtime in a red nightcap fit in a large yellow tub. Each figure can be removed and used as a roly-poly toy.

THREE MEN IN A TUB
Fisher-Price Toys

BLOCKS

Blocks are enormously important toys throughout childhood. There are a number of suitable kinds of blocks the young baby will enjoy. Now baby will simply handle them, getting used to the size and shape of the blocks. Cloth-covered, foam-rubber blocks are particularly good since they are noiseless, washable and soft without sharp edges. Lightweight, they are also excellent for throwing. Within the next few months, by baby's first birthday, he will be able to build a tower two to three blocks high.

• The TOYS TO GROW ON catalog offers one such set of cloth blocks from England. There are nine squares beautifully designed with simple, colorful pictures of animals, fruits, toys and other outdoor objects. Each cube features four different images of these familiar objects.

• CHICCO has designed a set of very soft plastic blocks. Each large block features a variety of designs and numbers imprinted on each side of the cube offering baby textured surfaces to touch and explore. In five pale colors, the blocks squeak when squeezed.

• F.A.O. SCHWARZ offers a set of six soft, hollow, rubber

blocks in solid colors each enclosing a whistle decorated with birds and animal figures.

• CHILDCRAFT's *Baby Blocks* are vinyl and foam cubes in bright colors with abstract designs of a boat, ball, train and a cat. Some of the blocks in the set contain a rattle or a chime.

• CHILD GUIDANCE *Cloth Cubes* are easy to grasp, soft and squeezable. They can be stacked to form a pattern of people, pets and other familiar figures. Another set of four cloth stacking blocks is illustrated with the cartoon character Hello Kitty doing her favorite thing—playing the violin, playing with blocks and trying on a hat.

Other good blocks for beginners are the set of bell-block rattles made by GALT. These two-inch wooden cubes with safely locked-in bells are the right size to grasp and chew. These blocks have been designed to help baby recognize shapes and colors. They are great for stacking.

There is a set of *Action Blocks* by SHELLCORE which has long been popular, and deservedly so. Each block is a single action toy in itself—one has a door to slide, another a ball to roll, others have a handle to turn, a dial to spin or a button to push. Each makes a special sound—a buzz, a jingle, a squeak or a ring. The variety may be overwhelming at first, so we suggest that you present one or two at a time. As your baby becomes used to the one motion and sound, add another.

It is best to settle down and play with the baby when you introduce the playthings that teach the early lessons in manipulation. Talk to him about each object, its features (color, shape, what the toy can do) and then give him time to try it on his own. Keep an eye on his progress with the toy. If he looks as if it is becoming too frustrating to handle, change the scene or the toy and come back to the game later. Remember, play is a child's work and toys are the tools. Parental involvement can assure a child's positive attitude towards play and the tools you will be offering. You, in essence, are your baby's first playmate and first experience with the art of playing. With your encouragement, he will joyously continue to experiment, to learn and to explore new horizons.

During these months you will notice that as your baby's fingers gain dexterity, he will develop powerful new interests. Not only will he point his forefinger at everything he sees, he will poke everything in sight—soft dolls, boxes, holes in his toys, your eyes, Dad's ears, Brother's face. And the idea that some objects can be put into other objects fascinates him. Stop and Think! An automatic motion for an adult or older child is a brand new experience for your baby. He is discovering dimension.

NESTING SETS

Many educational toy companies offer nesting sets at graduating levels of difficulty. The first sets are brilliantly colored plastic cups. The second are square "beakers" more difficult to nest because of the precise fitting required by the corners. The third are nested barrel halves which screw together, each forming a whole barrel and each then fitting into a larger barrel. These are generally recommended for eighteen months to three years. We suggest them at this early age because of the baby's interest in the insides of objects and the discovery of *in* and *out*. Give your baby a few of the cup shapes first. He will not actually nest them but will use them as manipulative toys, handling, and tasting them and poking a finger into them before he discovers that the smaller ones fit into bigger ones.

Most sets consist of between six and ten pieces—too many for the child to be able to perceive the graduations in size. To encourage nesting without pushing your baby beyond his capacity, it is a good idea to introduce him to only three of the pieces at first: the smallest, the largest and one middle-sized piece. He will discover the fitting relationships much sooner if the differences in size are this obvious.

With your help, baby will learn how to place the smaller cup into the larger cup. Once again, talk to him about size. Show him the various sizes so that he can see how one compares to the other. Some of the concepts he will begin to understand as he reaches nine months are:

ROCK-A-STACK
Fisher-Price Toys

- putting in; falling out
- empty and full
- closed and open
- side by side
- big, bigger, biggest
- small, smaller, smallest
- differences in basic, primary colors

When helping baby with nesting toys, add to the lesson by illustrating your classifications with a story he loves to hear—"The Three Little Pigs," "The Three Bears," or maybe "The Ten Little Indians."

A selection of nesting and stacking toys which will fulfill your baby's interest in putting things into and out of are:

• FISHER-PRICE's *Rock-A-Stack* has become a traditional first stacking toy for baby. Five graduated rings in colors of the rainbow (red, orange, yellow, green and blue) are placed on a center post in order of size. The stack rocks back and forth with a gentle push from baby.

• KIDDICRAFT offers another traditional nesting and stacking toy. *Barrels and Beakers*, in graduated sizes, come in vivid primary colors.

They nest into each other or stack upon one another. There are twelve beakers which can be stacked to form one large tower. This may be too much for baby to handle at first. So, build a smaller one of three beakers—perhaps all in one color. Then, keep adding a beaker and a color. Your child will soon comprehend size, order and color identification. Each beaker or barrel has an animal shape imprinted on the bottom.

STACKING PUPPY
Playskool

- PLAYSKOOL's *Stacking Puppy* is a charming stack toy with three rings which form the body of the puppy. The large green ring is placed in the boat base, then the yellow goes on, and, finally, a red ring becomes the base for the puppy's head. The entire stack rocks and, also, floats on water.

Playskool also presents *Baby's Basket*—a picnic basket with four fruit shapes, each designed to fit in its place on top of the yellow basket. Playskool's *Clown Stack* is a colorful circus clown wearing a four-colored ruffled collar which can be stacked in any order. Your baby can remove the clown's head and arrange the collar as he chooses. The Clown rocks while a bell rings within the safety post.

- THE FIRST YEAR's *Stack 'M Up Cups* come in eight different colors in graduated sizes. Each cup is numbered in order of size to help develop counting skills. They can be nested or stacked. The cups are simple yet versatile enough to be used in many ways during the next few months when baby is gathering information about color, numbers and sizes.

A variation on the *in* and *out* theme is found in these two toys:

- CHILD GUIDANCE's *Beep Beep Car*, baby's first car, is easy to handle and push along. The smiling driver comes in and out of the car. Your baby presses a red horn for attention. The car makes a clickity-click sound as he maneuvers it in and out of a make-believe garage.

- *The Chicken House* is a perfect first puzzle for a baby of this age. The see-through egg fits into the chicken which fits into a house where a ladybug and butterfly are playing hide and seek. Each part rattles and can also be used for teething.

BEEP BEEP CAR
Child Guidance

BATH TOYS

Now that your baby can sit up without support, he will really be having fun in his bath. The feel of the water against his skin, the ripples and little waves he kicks up and the beautiful splashing will make the bath a high point in his day. He will need to have a variety of bath-time playthings as well, and here too, there is a cornucopia to choose from.

Water play continues the ideas of movement and motion that baby has been learning and adding to his repertoire. Your baby can now learn all about the properties of another element—water. The way water feels—wet, warm or cool, the graceful flow, the easy way it moves about will be illustrated when he is put in his bath and uses his bath toys.

• CHILD GUIDANCE's companion activity to the *Busy Box* is *Busy Bath*. Like the crib version, this has proven to be one of your baby's favorite tub toys. What a delight when he pulls the handle. Swoosh! Water activates one of the many objects positioned on the board: water rocks the sailboat or spins the starfish or revolves the merry-go-round. Watch the dolphin gracefully squirt water into a cup. A pump action takes the water directly from the tub creating a non-stop flowing action.

BUSY BATH
Child Guidance

• CHILD GUIDANCE also offers *Tub Tykes*. Your child forms his own Navy with these three charming and smiling sailors who come in and out of three floating vessels—a life preserver, a turtle raft and a rowboat.

• FISHER-PRICE's *Bath Activity Center* is similar in concept to the Busy Bath. This active waterfront scene has water wheels, spinning dolphins and a very cute grinning octopus.

• FISHER-PRICE's *Splash & Stack Bluebird* is a unique bath toy. This five-piece toy, a big Bluebird, easily comes apart. The head is used as a pouring cup with the beak as the spout; the tail-feather section doubles as a funnel; the nest can be used as a water or sand strainer. The body, itself, becomes a large bowl which holds a soft yellow baby bird that squeaks and squirts.

Another joyous offering by the same company, smiling, rosy *Happy Apple*, rolls, chimes and floats—another wonderful bathtime companion.

• PLAYSKOOL's *Bath Bubbles*, both large and small sizes, contain a moving starfish or sea horse encased within a clear plastic bubble. Your baby can roll it or let the ball float on water while the sea animals flutter about.

TUB PETS
Playskool

• EARLY YEARS makes *Yellow Duck*, the perfect water companion. Another irresistible aquatic is Ernie's Sesame Street favorite, *Rubber Ducky*.

• PLAYSKOOL's *Tub Pets* are friendly and useful tub friends. This soft trio is covered in washable terry cloth and doubles as washcloths. The yellow duck, yellow fish and the blue and green turtle make bath time a happy experience.

• F.A.O. SCHWARZ's set of nineteen foam bathtub blocks is another good tub toy. These blocks stick together on contact and will not absorb water. The *Floating Family* package contains a green turtle, a blue pitcher and a boat holding a play family. All float and are fun to play with in the tub as well as out. They are also satisfying for baby to gum and chew.

Simpler and just as delightful, are the multiplicity of floating bath animals available everywhere. Any floating ball or a plastic cup from the kitchen will do nicely, but the baby will undoubtedly prefer little animals, especially if they squeak or spout water when squeezed. And don't overlook the fun of a small sponge that the baby can dip and squeeze, or a washcloth of his own so that he can imitate your motions.

SPLASH & STACK BLUEBIRD
Fisher-Price Toys

TEETHERS

The average baby will cut his first tooth in the middle of the lower gums at approximately seven months. Actually there really is no "average" baby, because each individual child has his own growth pattern. So the age will vary; the teething process, however, does go on throughout infancy up to about age two and a half, by which time he should have his full set of twenty baby teeth. Throughout this entire period, he *has* to bite, chew and gum to help relieve the discomfort. It is essential to provide him with a number of safe, pleasurable aids (sometimes called gummers), or you will find him gnawing on the furniture or gumming on the tail of the loyal, loving cat. Many rattles are also teethers, and you can bring them out again now, as well as any teethers you might have given him to play with earlier.

Any teether that the baby is going to be using when he is crawling or when he is likely to fall should be soft enough not to cause injury if he should fall on it. However, he needs very hard surfaces to press his gums against, and perhaps you will have to reserve these hard teethers for times when he is relatively confined in his high chair or bouncing seat.

There is a kind of teether available in drugstores that is designed to be refrigerated—this teether is filled with a liquid that holds the cold and helps soothe and numb the baby's sore gums. This sort of teether can be kept in the refrigerator or the freezer.

Gummers are generally soft, vinyl toys. There is a delightful set of three spiny, chewy, bright-colored *Hedgehogs* with funny little faces. Originally, the hedgehogs emitted a soft whistling sound when squeezed. However, when *Consumer Reports* pointed out the potential hazard of squeakers that could be removed and possibly swallowed, the squeakers were eliminated. In all toys for this age, metal insert squeakers should be avoided.

Don't laugh, but you can also find some fine teethers among dog toys! The bone-shaped hard rubber shapes with textured surface are particularly suitable. Be sure to pick dog toys that can be sterilized.

• FIRST YEARS' collection of teethers is an excellent assortment for baby: a string of soft teething beads in bright colors, a cool ring teether and a cool triangle teether (both of which help your baby soothe aching gums), and a *Sof'star* teether with four textured edges to let the child chew away to his delight.

• BERCHET's *Teething Toy* is a "Y"-shaped teether with each arm holding a different texture to explore. The revolving ball in the center adds further interest.

• CHILD GUIDANCE has a bendable *Teething Jack* in soft, yellow vinyl. This one also offers an interesting selection of textures on each corner for chewing, feeling and grabbing onto. Another popular product from this company is the *Cookie Monster* teething rattle. Safe to chew on, this Sesame Street pal fits perfectly into your baby's hand. He can shake the Cookie Monster to make a sound or press the yellow cookie he is holding for a happy squeaking sound.

• FISHER-PRICE has a collection of teethers and teething rattles that come in pretty colors in all shapes and sizes. The *Strawberry* and *Bunny* teethers are fun to use.

• PLAYSKOOL's *Happy Teethers* is another trio of brightly colored soft animals for chewing on. The Pink Turtle, Yellow Bear and Green Frog, each sitting atop a firm white teething ring, are wonderful just to play with.

• FISHER-PRICE's polyethylene *Snap-Lock Beads* are also good for chewing. This is a set of five shapes, including one with accordion-like ridges. They will pop apart and pop together again in different arrangements, so they come into a new usefulness on a higher level. After your baby is two, you can reintroduce them as a color- and shape-sorting learning device.

Some time between eight and ten months, your baby will be able to pull himself around and begin to creep (although some babies never do—one day they just stand up and walk). What a thrill it will be for him to be able to move around for himself! He will love getting into *everything*, so you had better prepare yourself for some pretty hectic times. Those calm, peaceful days of quiet playpen play are a thing of the past.

You will need to make very sure the entire house is safe for exploring, and you have to begin to exercise a great deal of patience, for he will probably exasperate you at times with his antics. Always bear in mind that what seems like naughty behavior is a necessary step in the direction of ultimate independence. Be firm and fair. To him, exploring and discovering everything for himself are his ways of learning about the world. He can't possible know right from wrong,

HAPPY TEETHERS
Playskool

SNAP-LOCK BEADS
Fisher-Price Toys

safe from dangerous or hot from cold until he experiences them. Your responsibility to him is to be always on guard against his harming himself, and then—let him go! Every stage of your child's development can be exciting and fun if you know what to expect of him.

BALLS

Once he is able to crawl a bit, he is ready for balls that he can go after. A marvelous innovation is the Clutch Ball. Variations of this ball are on the market in a variety of colors and materials. Most of them wheeze when squeezed, and all are perfect for holding, grasping, pushing, rolling and retrieving.

Tupperware makes an interesting multi-purpose ball with a long play life called *Shape-O*, which has ten openings, each of a different shape, through which objects of matching shapes can be inserted. Now the ball serves as a large rattle which is easy to hold and to pass from hand to hand. In another few months, when your baby creeps, he can roll the ball along the floor and go after it. Later, at about two years, it can be brought into use as a shape sorting device. At about three, the individual shapes can be used as clay or sand molds or you can roll out a little Play-Doh and use the shapes as cookie cutters. By the age of four, the numerals and corresponding number of dots on each shape make Shape-O useful for number and counting games.

• PLAYSKOOL's *Touch 'N Clutch Ball* is perhaps the most unusual and best clutch ball around. The ball's design is highly textured to encourage your baby's sense of touch. The two interlocking rings (one yellow, the other green) encircle a red ball which is also a rattle. Your child can easily grasp the edges of the rings to explore the various sensations the ball offers.

There is also a selection of textured balls covered in multi-colored cloth or terry. These are easy to roll about or throw across the playpen or for playing catch with Mom or Dad. Whatever your selection of rolling toys, the baby will continue to enjoy his storehouse of balls for many months to come, particularly when he starts to creep.

MUSCLE DEVELOPERS

Since this is the period of rapid growth of the heavy muscles of the torso, you should look for toys that will help this development along and simultaneously provide enjoyable play. CHILD GUIDANCE has produced the *Cookie Monster*, a loving figure mounted on swiveling ball casters. It is contoured to support the baby's body. He lies stomach-down on it, with his arms and legs free to swing about, thus offering him an opportunity to exercise his limbs and his back muscles

TOUCH 'N CLUTCH
Playskool

as he maneuvers around. This gives tremendous freedom to the child not yet able to crawl well on his own.

This type of device is best when the baby is pretty close to being able to crawl naturally. Don't be afraid that the Cookie Monster's usefulness will be short-lived. Two- and three-year olds love to sit on it and scoot around the house.

There are several types of bouncing, swinging and rocking seats which can be introduced between six and nine months. The Teeter is a hardwood rocker with a seat and security bar to keep the baby from falling out. Its suspension spring action allows the child to rock or bounce safely and without supervision. This rocker is available in toy and juvenile furniture stores.

Slightly more expensive is the *Rocker-Spinner* (Creative Playthings) or *Rock-N-Spin* (Childcraft) which combine the back-and-forth and the round-about motions. The seat is mounted on a saucer-like base, and the baby can rock in any direction by his own movement, or with help he can enjoy the novel experience of spinning about. He will enjoy this seat until the age of two, by which time he will be able to accomplish the spinning motion unaided.

Exclusive to F.A.O. Schwarz and expensive is the *Horse Shoo-Fly*. This wooden horse, less than two feet high, has a cross-bar to hang onto and should delight baby well into his third year.

There are also bouncer-walkers, usually with sling seats of canvas or flexible plastic, which have the spring suspension that provides the bouncing action, have legs on casters, but no foot base. As your baby stretches his feet down to the floor, his natural urge to push moves him forward (or backward) in an early approximation of the movement he will later use for walking. In selecting one of these pre-walking bouncers, be sure the base is wide, so that it cannot tip over. Be sure there is a plastic bumper all the way around the base of the bouncer-walker so that your baby cannot get too close to furniture. This is not so much to protect the furniture as it is to protect your child from bumped legs and mashed fingers. Thayer has several models available which meet these standards.

The baby, although a long way from walking alone, will adore the out-of-doors and all the sights, sounds and smells of the outside world. You and he may be tired of daily outings in the cumbersome carriage. Perhaps a light stroller or one of the newer baby carriers—a canvas seat in an aluminum frame that straps to your back—would be more practical. The *Gerry Carriers* are the best known and are very well made. Infants seem to love these snug yet wide-open "cockpits," but if you have any doubts about being able to support your baby's weight on your back, try it on with him in it before you buy.

By the time the child is nine months old, he is well on the way to being a participating member of the family. He's becoming very social and will differentiate between family faces and those of strangers. He gets excited in anticipation of his meals—and angry if they are delayed. He is gaining an awareness that his environment can be controlled, sometimes by himself. He is generally self-contained, self-satisfied and capable of amusing himself for reasonable periods of time.

He is beginning to vocalize more, "talking" to his toys and reacting with increasing responsiveness to conversation. He will soon be able to associate words with actions and will begin to enjoy action games like pat-a-cake and "This little piggy went to market." Under your watchful eye, he will move out into the world from his restricted crib and playpen. Keep him occupied with some of the playthings we have suggested and give him every opportunity to learn by exploring with his hands and body.

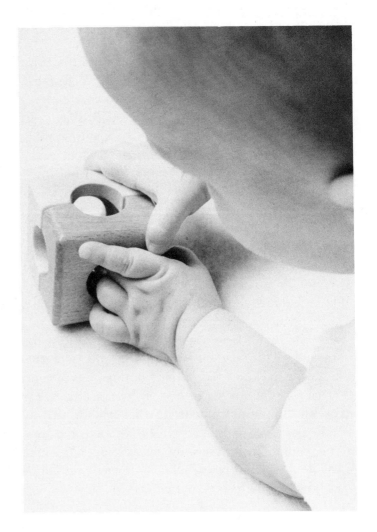

Nine to Twelve Months
Ending an Amazing Year

Dr. Arnold Gesell wrote, "The developmental transformations which occur in the first year of life far exceed those of any other period excepting only the period of gestation."

You have seen how your baby has gained command of his eyes and hands and learned to use them in coordination. You have also seen how he has gained greater command of his body and is beginning to move around under his own power. During this last period of his first year, your baby's biggest accomplishment will be getting himself up on his own two feet to a standing position. He may have trouble sitting back down again once he is upright, but he will soon learn, and in short order will be cruising around the house, holding on to furniture and walls for support in preparation for that all-important first step alone.

But don't rush him. Let him take each new stage of development at his own speed. Some children are quite happy to creep for a long while and may not walk before a year and a half. Others may walk as early as nine months. Don't be alarmed if your child seems slower than his contemporaries; your pediatrician will let you know if there is any cause for concern.

These months just before your child's first birthday will be a time of intense motor activity. He will now be scooting about and poking into anything within reach. Now you must be very sure your home is baby-proof—for the child's sake and yours, too. Take particular care to put away delicate or breakable household objects, all pills and other medicines, cleansers and sprays, loose buttons, safety pins and whatever else that could be swallowed.

Make sure electric outlets are covered, lamp cords are out of the way and rugs are secured. Tablecloths are a common hazard—if the baby tries to pull himself up by the overhanging edge, you may find a hurt child as well as Grandma's china in a million pieces. It goes without saying that knives and other sharp or pointed instruments must never be left lying around. Use your common sense and examine your house with great care for anything that might be harmful. This year-old child is very alert and his curiosity is boundless, so be on the lookout all the time.

The main thing to remember in connection with the exploratory period is that your baby is learning about the world through touching, handling and mouthing everything. And you want to encourage his curiosity and not keep saying "no, no!" to every learning effort he makes. Ideally, your house or apartment should be arranged so that you need to say "no" only to permanent hazards, such as the hot stove, which cannot be removed.

It is a very good idea, if at all possible, to have a special play area set aside for your baby. A corner of a room—possibly blocked off by furniture or a gate—where he can move about freely and without danger will do nicely. You child will want to be near you, and probably the most convenient play area will be in or close to the kitchen where you probably spend most of your time (but not within reach of the stove or oven). He will like to play quietly near you while you go about your daily chores. He will also observe the routines and activities of other family members with great fascination. You can be sure your baby is picking up all kinds of information and sensations as he carefully studies people and what they do.

However, while there are limits to impose for the safety of the child, too many restrictions (i.e. keeping him within the confines of his playpen during a great part of his playtime) can lead to boredom and can discourage your baby from following his natural instinct to learn, explore and experiment.

Your baby is becoming ever more of a companion, and you can expect an exciting developmental milestone soon: his first word! The chances are your baby will begin to show a real interest in rudimentary "conversations" and will listen carefully to them and try to produce a few words of his own. As Dr. Benjamin Spock points out, "Talking seems to be largely a matter of temperament or personality." Outgoing, friendly children are eager to communicate, whereas the more serious, contemplative child may observe the world for a long time before he has any comment to make.

Dorothy Corkille Briggs writes about the importance of learning how to speak in her book, *Your Child's Self-Esteem.* "Language is the tool that finally allows the baby to feel fully separate. When he learns his name he has a symbol for thinking of himself apart from others."

Experiments with infants suggest that the degree of warm responsiveness that parents and others caring for your baby provide, forms the foundation for a future positive view of self.

"Parents who never play with their infants or who care for them with a cold efficiency fail to give their infants an early impression of their importance," Ms. Briggs writes.

Language learning accelerates during these next few months. Your child is now beginning to grasp the context of words: bird with sky, a dog and barking, music and the radio. He may not yet be able to say very much, but he will probably understand a great many things you say to him. He communicates with you through gestures, babbling, pointing, body movement and even shouting. He will undoubtedly launch his own dialogue by saying "Mama" or "Dada" as has nearly every baby before him. Soon, as his first birthday approaches, he will be able to say one or two words and will be waving "bye-bye" to the delight of his family and friends. Correct pronunciation will be lacking for a time, but baby will make up for it through the sheer enjoyment of imitating a sound or a word he hears.

Your baby will love to hear all sorts of pleasant sounds. In fact, he will respond to the tone of a person's voice with his whole being. An angry or bored voice will make him feel sad. Such a tone may even make him feel as if he has done something *wrong*, something to make you feel negative towards him. A happy, enthusiastic, pleasant approach (difficult as it may be to remain in such a mood when you are busy and preoccupied with other things) is worth the effort because it encourages your baby to go on with his endeavors.

FIRST BOOKS

Songs and rhymes, at times the sillier the better, encourage him to speak rhythmically. As the baby's use of language begins, the time comes to introduce books.

First books should be made either of heavy cardboard or cloth so that baby can handle them easily, chew on them or fling them about if he wishes. They should have one large picture on each page with an identifying word on the opposite page, so that you can show him the relationship between words and objects. He won't be able to "read" the word but he will like to look at the colorful pictures and point to them in recognition. As he thumbs through a soft cover book, he will usually turn a few pages at one time. The board books are written especially with this age group in mind. There is no need to worry about ripped pages and they can be wiped off when they get dirty.

This is a wonderful time to establish a reading-together routine. Set aside a quiet part of the day—afternoon or bedtime, snuggle up with baby on your lap and explore the wonderful contents of a book. Since he loves to imitate the sounds he hears, point to the picture and tell him about the object shown on the page. Show him an example of the object in the room—his ball, a doll, the bed, Daddy. As he grows, so will his approach to the book. Now he is a bit passive as you read to him. Soon he will be turning the pages to reach a drawing he remembers. Then he will energetically point to the object in the book and identify it with one in his room. One day, he will be reading this book to you. A lifelong enjoyment has begun!

The popular PLATT & MUNK books, *Baby's First Toys* and *Baby's Things*, are excellent and are available at most dime stores in cloth or in spiral-bound cardboard. Also suitable now are the block books (Western Publishing) that look just like wooden blocks until the heavy cardboard pages are opened. Avoid books with impressionistic illustrations or with many objects on a page. Your baby is still figuring out very basic ideas about what things are and what they look like. Also avoid paper pages until the baby can turn them without accidentally tearing them.

• The BRIMAX board books feature two series that your baby will enjoy. These are designed and illustrated to enable baby to identify as well as relate to the familiar objects he will read about. Each page has been laminated and is easy to keep clean. The *Show Baby* series cover everyday events in your baby's routine—Mealtime, Playtime, Bedtime, Bathtime. Each book shows an item (the pajamas) simply illustrated. The facing page describes how this item will be used (put on nice warm pajamas).

• LADYBIRD books from England have been delighting babies for ages. *Baby's First Book* is filled with lovely pictures of objects baby may see everyday and is learning to use.

• PRICE/STERN/SLOAN publish another *Baby's First Books* that show large full-color drawings printed on board stock. The background is printed in a bright, primary color which sets the scene for the illustration shown. Subjects offered are: Looking At Animals, Going For A Ride, In The House, At The Table.

• DICK BRUNA's cloth books feature beautiful, bold pictures of familiar objects. The illustrations are printed on boldly colored fabric. There are no words. The pictures about Eating, Dressing, Counting, Working tell the story.

Animals especially appeal to baby.

• Richard Scarry's *Lowly Worm Book* (RANDOM HOUSE) is a popular one with its clear and clever drawings about Lowly Worm's possessions.

• HOUGHTON MIFFLIN's *Paddington Helps Out* and *Paddington At Large* by Michael Bond relate the adventurous tales of every child's favorite bear. In this case, your baby can hold onto a stuffed Paddington while listening to his escapades.

• *Baby Bear* books by Eric Hill (RANDOM HOUSE) are filled with pictures of everyday things found in familiar places: The Park, At Home, Up There, My Pets.

• JOHNSON & JOHNSON have developed a series of Activity Books which allow the baby to bring his book to life. The main character can be fitted into various slots in the books—on a chair, in the bath, in bed, your baby can open windows and doors. Each story deals with baby's daily activities—teaches him about friendship, taking a bath or going to bed. There are three stories available: *Baby Bear Plays At Home, Wet Willy's Water Fun, Sleepy Bunny Goes To Bed*. The books of soft vinyl are flexible and easy to keep clean. Each has a handle so that your baby can carry it around with him. This series is a nice change from the usual board or cloth books, adding a third dimension to reading activity.

ACTIVITY BOOKS
Johnson & Johnson

At first your child will enjoy looking at the figures with you. Then as he gets a little older, you name each object in the book or name the color of the page and count the numbers of items shown. He will be absorbing this information for future use.

Parents expect baby to respond to their efforts on his behalf, as they try to entertain him or teach him with songs, facial expressions and toys. But, more and more infant researchers are finding that it is most beneficial if we learn how to *respond* to our children's actions and verbal expressions.

When he holds up a toy for you to see, show your enthusiasm; when he points to an object across the room and babbles "Mama", tell him how clever he is. From this moment on the baby will be initiating playful moments and leading you by the hand to show you the wonderful things he has discovered. What we may take for granted as adults are *brand new, first time* experiences for him.

Your response to his developing sociability is crucial to his later social development. An easygoing, friendly and loving parent who lets his child know how much fun he is to be with can expect a warm, trusting child with an enormous will to grow, mature and to enjoy life.

Your child is more fun to play with than you ever could have imagined. Baby loves to play games, all kinds of games. They challenge his increasing awareness and intelligence. Hide a ball under a cover and let him find it. Roll the ball towards him and play catch. Wrestle with him, bounce him on your knee, get down on the floor and help him build a stack of blocks. Baby will place the two he can manage on top of each other. You add the rest to the tower. Then, a tap of his hand will send them all tumbling down. He absolutely adores dropping *everything* he can. His sense of humor at this age is very keen. Don't miss sharing this fun-to-be-alive feeling with him.

He will delightedly pat his image in a mirror as well as want to play pat-a-cake, "Where's the doggie? *There's* the doggie!" and "How big is Baby? So big!" (holding his hand to the top of his head). He will not only want to play them, he will want to play them endlessly. You will both enjoy simple, rhythmic nursery games, and he will love being sung to, played with, being danced about and frolicked with.

There are a number of nursery rhyme books available, two with special games to play:

• GOLDEN PRESS's *Play With Me* by Esther Wilkin, is a lovely first picture book filled with traditional rhymes and games to play with your baby. Each page illustrates a different game. One game is played while holding baby in your arms:

"Mommy's (Daddy's) arms are a little boat,
A-sailing we will go,
We'll sail-a-boat, sail-a-boat, sail-a-boat fast,
We'll sail-a-boat, sail-a-boat, sail-a-boat slow."

• PENGUIN BOOKS' *This Little Puffin* is another enchanting collection of musical games, action songs, and finger plays compiled by Elizabeth Matterson. From the chapter on "Games to Play with Baby":

"Two little eyes to look around,
Two little ears to hear each sound;
One little nose to smell what's sweet,
One little mouth that likes to eat."

(Point to each feature as it is mentioned.)

PEG TOYS

It is interesting to observe how your child has developed the way in which he holds onto objects. At seven months, he dropped the toy he was holding to reach for another. Then, at ten months, he gingerly took the second toy offered in his free hand without dropping the first. If he had been given a third object, he would have had to let go of one to accept the new item. Now, at twelve months of age, if offered a third toy he would find a way to hang onto all three. He may put one of the first two in the crook of the opposite arm, taking the new toy with the free hand. As long as he can figure out where to put the extras, he will continue to accept more and more toys.

Your baby is now a competent tool user. He is capable of reaching for and getting a toy without help from the parent. Most babies of this age use the right hand as the "active explorer" and the left as a container and holder. Research conducted at Harvard's Center for Cognitive

Studies showed that infants are able to push up and hold a sliding see-through trap door with one hand while reaching inside for a toy with the other.

The child's command of his arms and hands is becoming increasingly sure. He works his fingers independently, and he can operate his index finger and thumb as pincers for more complicated manipulative tasks. His ever-probing index finger pokes and explores holes, hollows, grooves and textures, and he will show an increasing interest in the small details on his toys and other objects he examines.

The baby is learning all about the characteristics of objects: their sizes and shapes; what they can do (such as roll around); whether they are heavy or light, smooth or rough, hot or cold. Everything your child touches still has to pass the "taste" test.

Your baby has spent almost a year gathering all sorts of information about himself and the world and other human beings. Now he is "ready, willing and able to learn, absorb and develop. It is up to you (the parent) to furnish the necessary stimuli, tools and encouragement," writes Dr. Eden in *Positive Parenting*.

Although most peg toys should not be used until after the child has mastered the ring-on-the-dowel action, we are suggesting you introduce your baby to one made by BRIO because of the tremendous importance peg toys play in the development of a child's coordination.

Most of them are so simple in appearance that they look dull and unexciting to adults who are unaware of the importance of the coordination skill required to fit the peg into the hole. The peg toy is the forerunner of shape-discrimination toys (such as shape sorters and jigsaw puzzles), and the skill it develops is the first of progressively more complex perceptual skills which culminate in the child's ability to read.

• BRIO's *Shapes And Colours* pegboard will consolidate your baby's new abilities to group objects by size, color and shape. It will help your child to begin to bring together all the elements of manipulation, sorting out and using the concepts of *in* and *out* that he has been experimenting with these past few months.

The nine slots on the wooden base are divided into three different shapes to hold a variety of pegs in graduated sizes. The three blue triangles, three yellow squares and three red round pegs are colorful and inviting to try. Play with your baby, encouraging him to put all the blue colors together. Then, see if he can match the square shape to the square shape on the board. Help him identify big, bigger and biggest as you line up the three different sizes of wooden shapes. Remember, this is an introduction to a number of concepts. Let him experiment with the pegboard at his own pace.

SHAPES AND COLOURS
BRIO

During the next year, this particular toy will clearly demonstrate just how your child's abilities and perceptions of color and size develop. As each month passes, his approach to the toy will change until he can easily and quickly match shape to shape, size to size and color to color.

SCANCRAFT has available three peg toys that offer practice in the area of developing manipulative skills. Their catalog features high quality wooden toys made in Scandinavia by award-winning manufacturers. The following toys were made by JUKKA.

• *The Dumper* is an attractive first car for baby. Made of natural wood, its edges have been rounded to a smooth finish so it is safe to handle. The bright red peg "driver" can be put into and taken out of his car.

• *The Passenger Car* holds six colorful passengers in red, green and yellow. They too can be moved in and out of their seats. Baby can learn to match the peg people by pairs of colors or can mix them about.

• *Putt-Putt Train* is an engine and two-car set, in all natural wood, with a peg-shaped engineer and two peg passengers.

• JOHNSON & JOHNSON makes *Fitting Forms*, an interesting toy that is a puzzle as well as a fitting toy. There are two soft, peg-shaped people—one sporting a red heart and the other a red star—that can be stacked, fitted in and out of a blue-boat base, and that can also double as hand puppets. There is a square block and a round rattling block that fit into the toy two different ways. This rewarding toy offers the toddler the opportunity to perfect eye-hand coordination through the experience of fitting shapes into their proper places.

PUTT-PUTT TRAIN
JUKKA

EXPLORATORY TOYS

If you have not already purchased or received a nesting set for your baby, he will enjoy one now and in the months to come. Bring out the nesting sets described in the previous chapter.

• CHILDCRAFT has a particularly interesting set called the *Lighthouse Stacker*. This six-piece stacking toy is assembled by fitting together matching geometric shapes molded onto the bottom of each piece. When properly fitted the individual beakers are transformed into a colorful lighthouse.

In addition to the baby's increased manipulative skills, he will be developing much more sophisticated mental processes. He is beginning to understand concepts, and the future scientist, lawyer, mathematician or artist is prefigured in this period of mental awakening. *In* and *out*, *together* and *apart*, *side* by *side*, *full* and *empty*, *hollow* and *solid*—all are fascinating and difficult ideas for him to take in, and, for the first time, he is beginning to make distinctions among them.

He even begins to perceive the difference between *one* and *two* or *more*. As his sense of perspective develops, the world doesn't look as flat as it did before. The third dimension begins to emerge as he raises himself to a vertical position and gradually begins to understand that some things are *in front of* or *behind* others or are *within reach* or *far away*. These are all very difficult relations to master. You are helping him by offering him a stimulating environment that encourages his exploration of the world of ideas.

FISHER-PRICE's *Discovery Cottage* enhances exploration and discovery play. Since your child is fast becoming a whiz at finding hidden objects he has so cleverly placed around the house, he will thoroughly enjoy this fun-filled cottage. There are over 13 play features: The front door makes a "ratcheting" sound when opened; push the round bulb to ring the front doorbell. The garage door becomes a ramp when opened. Over-size *Play Family* figures—a puppy and an infant—can be gently dropped down the chimney to come sliding out of the side of the cottage. Or, they can be popped onto the red tricycle and given a ride. The roof lifts up to reveal a baby's room with a mirror inside. Voila! Baby discovers a familiar face—his!

DISCOVERY COTTAGE
Fisher-Price

From nine to twelve months, the child will still continue to enjoy many of the toys you may have given him already, and he will be able to play with them with new fascination and concentration. His collection of balls will be a special treat as he creeps around after them. He will also like to sit facing you and play rolling the ball back and forth.

Creepers like all sorts of rolling toys, cans, oatmeal boxes and especially, the five-and-ten-cent store novelty cylinders powered by rubber-banded mechanisms. Your baby rolls the cylinder away and is just delighted when it returns. But the toys that do not return are preferable because they encourage the baby to do more creeping to reach them again. A small toy that your baby can hold and then roll along the floor while he creeps is perfect for this age.

His bath toys will delight him still, and soft blocks will be used for more intense play as he tries to stack them, fails, puts one next to the other, picks it up, throws it, scoots after it, all the while seeing *what* they will do as he manipulates them. You might consider introducing him to a more durable set of hard rubber blocks or a set of hand-sized wooden cubes at this point.

He will be absolutely enchanted with the household objects you give him. A set of colorful plastic mixing bowls, a box or basket full of wooden clothespins (not the pinching kind) to finger, empty out and put back in, a large cardboard box to crawl into, wooden kitchen spoons and especially pots and pans to bang—these will be lots of fun at no expense.

STACK & FIT SCHOOL
Johnson & Johnson

WEE WHEELS
Child Guidance

Just the right toy to introduce now is JOHNSON & JOHNSON's *Stack and Fit School*—it provides intriguing combinations of activities. This color-coded, fitting, stacking, nesting and sorting toy helps teach organizing and sorting skills involving size, shape and color. Shapes in bright colors can be used to build a tower on top of the school house base. Or, they can be nested and fitted together. The child can practice eye-hand coordination by fitting tubes inside square shapes, then placing the squares into rectangular shapes which, in turn, all fit neatly into the school house box. Pieces can be matched by color and sorted by size.

A first car you might consider for the almost-one-year old is AMBI's *Baby's First Car*. The car is easy to push along. Watch the eyes (windows) blink as your child rolls it across the floor. Press the red light bulb on top for a warning "squeak, squeak" as the yellow car comes racing across the room.

• CHILD GUIDANCE's *Wee Wheels* has a special design that makes these cheery yellow vehicles (truck, train and car) ideal for use as baby's first hand-powered car. Built to fit small hands, the cabs of each vehicle have an easy-to-grasp handle to hold onto when pushing or holding. The smooth, rounded edges are safe to use for teething. When baby picks one up, it makes a rattling sound.

Other surprise toys that would delight your baby now include the classic jack-in-the-box.

The importance of toys such as this one go far beyond their amusement value. The baby is still learning that things he cannot see are not really gone. This is why he sometimes frets when you leave the room and why he so enjoys games like peek-a-boo or "Where's the baby?" When you hide your face behind a blanket or behind your hands and then suddenly reveal it, your baby squeals with pleasure to see you again. You really are there. The jack-in-the-box is a toy which helps him to grasp this idea.

Some babies are frightened by the suddenness of these jacks that jump on springs. It is a good idea to start with one of the gentler versions.

• AMBI's *Jack-In-The-Ball* produces a smiling face popping out of what at first seems to be a brightly colored ball. When your baby pushes on the yellow button, a clown comes up making a squeaking sound. Push the clown down and the toy becomes a ball again. The fully opened figure can be used as a roly-poly toy that your child can carry around with him on his travels.

By the end of this period, you will be getting ready for the baby's first birthday. His growth is one of the most exciting experiences the family will have, and the first birthday is a good time to begin keeping a permanent height record. Now that he can stand up, you can mark your baby's height at regular intervals. There are many attractive measuring charts available, and, of course, you can make your own. Try to provide for permanent markings, as your child will be most interested in his growth in later years.

When you think back on it, this has truly been an amazing year. The marvelous, tiny, helpless creature you were presented with at birth can now do a great many things by himself. He can say a few words, he is preparing to walk and he is a curious and tireless explorer of his environment. As he strikes out to discover a brand new world, you are his guide for wonderful adventures in an ever-expanding universe of experiences.

Twelve to Fifteen Months
"I Can Walk!"

Happy Birthday! A yummy looking cake is placed before your baby. One lone candle is the main attraction. Cameras are poised. Baby blows! Hurrah! The infant is now a toddler, an individual with a distinct personality.

Now you will be dealing with a little person who can communicate likes and dislikes, wishes and needs. The toddler begins to move independently into a world of his own. The three main areas of growth during the next year involve organization, initiative and originality. All qualities are required as the child grows into adulthood. As a toddler develops, he is putting himself together in increasingly complex ways. As each stage is mastered the foundation for the next step in development is set in place.

The world takes on a new perspective now that the toddler can stand and walk. He can see more at one time—the tops of tables, for instance, and what is on them when he is standing in his crib. He will spy a favorite toy across the floor. Then, without waiting, he will be able to go and get it. He is independent, impulsive, self-assertive, curious and adventuresome. he is now discovering *self* and just what he *can do by himself.*

This new-found independence might suggest that baby no longer needs his mother or father as much as he did during the first year. But, the toddler needs parental assurance more than ever. He will constantly come back to home base for a bit of praise and parental admiration. According to Dr. Stanley I. Greenspan, "The key thing in dealing with toddlers is for the child to sense this admiration in the eyes of the parents. When there is no praise from the parent, there is no joy for the child."

At this stage of development, the toddler is also laying the foundation for many skills needed to achieve success during the school years:

> verbal confidence
> ability to solve problems
> curiosity and enthusiasm
> sociability and control of emotions

You and his toys will provide him with the outlets needed to practice and experiment with these growing abilities.

Dolls and soft animals allow for make-believe play, encouraging verbal exchange as well as feelings of tenderness and care. He talks to his dolls in the way you speak to him. He hugs and kisses them in the way that he has been hugged and kissed.

Picture books help the toddler identify objects and colors. Looking at picture books and being read to at bedtime create an excitement for books, now, and all literature, later, that will last a lifetime. The interchange between you and the baby helps him practice many details of his development. Listening to you and looking at the illustrations enhances sensory capacities; turning the pages by himself will aid fine motor coordination.

Your baby is solving problems a mile a minute, and pegboards are valuable in the area of problem solving. Sorting and putting objects into categories by shape, size and color prepare him for the future techniques he will need in many school testing programs. SAT's watch out! Sorting by size begins mathematical thinking.

Cause-and-effect toys help in the development of intellectual learning. "Now, why did that happen?" he asks himself. "Let's find out!"

Indoor gyms and riding toys are just right for exercising large muscles. Toddlers can explore their surrounding territory with great enthusiasm when offered this type of mobility.

Musical and rhythm games or dancing to a record not only give an enjoyable feeling, but also help the toddler gain confidence as he acquires body control.

Give him crayons and plenty of paper and room to spread out and scribble to help with dexterity. The practice with the crayon prepares for the use of a pencil or pen later on. The toddler's *impressions* as he makes his marks on the paper, build self-confidence since these colorfully imprinted images come from within his own thoughts and imagination.

Sometime during the next few months you can look forward to a glorious moment: your baby's first step. Try to have a camera on hand to preserve that unforgettable accomplishment.

He will probably plop right back down again and be quite frustrated until he is steady enough to get going on his own. Before you know it, however, your baby will have graduated into his first pair of real shoes and be toddling around with great glee as fast as he can go.

Dr. Spock points out that "You don't have to do anything to teach a child to walk. When his muscles, his nerves, and his spirit are ready you won't be able to stop him."

That first birthday will not only be a landmark, it will undoubtedly also be a great deal of fun, for another wonderful trait has begun to flower—a sense of humor. The child is a great imitator now, mimicking your speech and actions. He will really play to his audience, if laughed at and encouraged. Do everything you can to stir his participation in communication by playing little games with him, singing simple songs, reciting nursery rhymes, pointing out sights (and identifying them) on his outings and bringing him into the life of the family as much as possible.

He won't respond coherently as yet, but he will be taking everything in and doing his best to react in his way to your attentions. He will love offering his toys to you (but will want them right back!); he will delight in scrambling on and off the furniture and creeping up and down stairs or scooting across the floor or yard with you in hot pursuit.

It is vitally important now that your child have an opportunity to engage in active play that will exercise the big muscles of his arms, legs and back. This exercise contributes not only to his physical development but also to his mental development. In early years, most of a child's learning comes through his senses, and the development of mind and body are closely interwoven.

As we have remarked, the big event in your child's life between twelve and fifteen months is his new-found ability to walk. His first steps will, of course, be very unsure ones, and he will probably fall a great deal before he is steady enough to do any serious walking on his own.

PUSH TOYS

Once he has his feet planted firmly on the ground, the right toys make walking even more fun. Push toys are particularly good. They give the beginning walker something to lean against as added support. The push toy makes a good transition from holding onto an immovable wall or chair to walking all alone. A small, wagon-type toy with a long handle is the best choice because he can steady himself as he pushes the vehicle along. Later, the cart can be used for play in transporting his things around the house or yard. Some versions come equipped with a set of blocks that fit into the cart itself.

• The CHILDCRAFT *First Wagon* is a strong push and pull wagon especially built for the toddler. A low wheelbase prevents tipping. A stationary handle gives the child steady hold-on support as he attempts those first steps. The hardwood wagon can also be loaded with his personal possessions.

• CHILD GUIDANCE's *Walk-Along Block Wagon* is another long-lasting hardwood wagon which doubles as a walker when the long handle is adjusted. Position the handle straight up and the wagon is ready for your baby to hold onto for balance. When the handle is set at an angle, the toddler can use it as a block wagon. The wagon is filled with 24 brightly colored hardwood blocks in four shapes and four colors.

• KIDDICRAFT's *Baby Walker* is the most appealing push toy we have seen. It is also the most imaginative. The beautifully colored red racing car, sporting large yellow wheels holds a dashing driver in a blue helmet. He moves up and down as your baby pushes the racer along an imaginary track. There are six yellow blocks stashed in front of the driver that can be removed and stacked and the movement of the car produces a clicking engine noise.

• PLAYSKOOL's push vehicle takes the form of a *Big Yellow Taxi*. In bright colors with a painted-on Panda driver, the taxi doubles as a toy box. Dolls or stuffed animals can go for a ride in the front seat. There is a roomy storage compartment for your child's other treasures. The taxi makes a clicking sound as it is pushed along. Playskool's *Giraffe Walker* has been a favorite push toy/walker for some years. This smiling, bright-eyed giraffe with red spots has a back support and handlebar ears to hold onto so that your baby can use it as a riding toy.

• TOYS TO GROW ON catalog features a luxurious *Push-Along, Ride-Along Bear* that is scaled for toddlers. When he tires of pushing the bear, the toddler can hop on his soft, plush back and get a push from you. The stuffed bear is supported on a solid steel frame with non-skid wheels and wide foot rests. This one can be expensive—a gift from Grandpa, perhaps.

• BERCHET's *Sand Walker* combines two activities baby loves to do at this age—toddling along outdoors and digging in dirt or sand. This red, yellow and blue vehicle conveniently holds four digging tools for use at the beach or in the garden.

RIDING TOYS

Riding toys differ from the walkers in that the baby actually sits astride a centerpiece. There are many riders on the market ranging from animal shapes to transportation-type toys. Introduce only the simplest of riding toys now. Pick one that is sized to your baby's height so that he can easily reach the floor and propel himself forward. This toy helps develop a mastery of large muscle skills.

LITTLE BROWN PONY
Playskool

A riding toy gives the toddler confidence about locomotion if he is not too steady on his feet as yet. Make certain that the seats are fitted and snug so that he won't topple off. The wheels should be secure to the frame of the vehicle and the base should be broad so that the toy won't tip over easily.

• PLAYSKOOL has two fun-to-ride figures:

Little Brown Pony, an appealing companion with a soft, plush coat and a tuft of yellow mane. His saddle and coat slip off for washing. When the pony moves, its large yellow wheels make a "clippety-clop" sound.

Popper School Bus is a familiar sight to toddlers who may see one just like it pick up neighborhood kids each morning. This version shows a smiling driver and his dog taking a bus load of waving children to school. Pop-pop balls in the front of the bus make the sound of the motor as the bus moves. Under the seat is a roomy storage area for personal possessions.

RIDING HORSE
Fisher-Price

• WONDER makes several interesting types of animal-shaped riding toys that your child will enjoy. *Bucky the Wonder Horse* is a brightly colored riding horse with quite a twinkle in his eye. He whinnies when the toddler pulls on his reins and bucks when the handles are pushed down. A storage compartment is hidden under the red saddle. *Roarin' Tiger Rider*, a loveable, smiling tiger is ready and roaring to go. When the child pushes down on the hold-on handles he is greeted by a friendly roar. *Barnaby Puppy* is another friendly pet with floppy ears and a hard-to-resist smile that says, "Come and play with me." *Buggy Bee* is a charming, cheerful-looking critter with a colorful body that rests on a six-wheel base. Green antennae serve as handle bars.

• FISHER-PRICE's *Riding Horse* features a vividly colored red seat which is specially shaped to hold the toddler securely on the horse. The red wheels make a "clippety-clop" sound as it rolls along. There is a built-in storage tray. Your baby can give the horse a ride by pushing the handle attached to the back of the seat.

• BERCHET offers baby the *Baby Roller*, a riding toy with a unique modern design that is a truly different kind of vehicle. Basically, it is a terrific looking steam roller with six large blue wheels, a bright red seat and yellow steering wheel. The seat lifts for storage.

• LITTLE TIKES takes great care when designing riding toys for the toddler. Geared to the way a toddler loves to move about, their riders are built for stability and easy maneuverability. *Little Red Rider* is a modern, sleek-looking red-and-white riding vehicle with a low center of gravity and wide wheel base to prevent tipping. The front wheels, unique in design, are very easy to steer. They can't go in the wrong direction. The saddle style seat has a high back for balance. (Little Tikes has imprinted a toll free 800 number on the underside of each toy as a

BUCKY THE WONDER HORSE
Wonder

LITTLE RED RIDER
Little Tikes

customer service feature. They welcome comments from customers who, in many instances, have influenced changes in old products and in the creation of new products.)

You will notice that many of these exciting riding toys make a noise. There is a good reason why they all have their own special sound. Children love noise, all kinds of noise. It seems to feed their sense of power. As your baby rides his horse, tiger or vehicle, something very exciting happens. His toy comes alive. It sounds just like the real car or horse he has seen on journeys to the supermarket.

ROCKERS

In addition to the riding toy, the toddler may also enjoy a rocker. This type of toy helps to develop balance and gross motor skills as he uses his whole body to push back and forth.

• FISHER-PRICE's *Rocking Puppy* is a happy, frolicky pet. This puppy has a specially designed seat and rockers that prevent over-rocking without curtailing all the fun. The puppy's paws serve as footrests and it makes a soft jingling sound as it moves. Soft plush ears and big blue eyes make the puppy seem very real to your baby.

• LITTLE TIKES' *Toddle-Tune Rocker* is a cheerful creature with red mop-top hair. Your baby holds onto a red bar as he rocks away to the pleasant sound of chimes.

• F.A.O. SCHWARZ's *Panda Rocker* is a beautifully designed toy from Trupa of Italy. The Panda's seat is also specially designed to hold baby firmly. Although expensive, the quality of this soft, plush and huggable Panda makes it a special gift.

• SCHOWANEK offers two distinctive versions of the wooden rocking horse. The *Little Carriage Horse* features a full chair with a cheerful-looking horse's head mounted in front of the seat. The other design is the traditional rocking horse. Both horses have thick, white manes. Either one gives your baby a rocking motion.

At this stage, when your baby is gaining his feet, he needs to be outdoors as much as possible, weather permitting. The ideal situation can be a fenced-in play area in your back yard, but city-dwellers will have to resort to parks and safe playgrounds where the baby can be protected from hazards and yet be able to move freely. Although he will be very unsteady and take many tumbles, what scientists call his gross motor drive (that is, the need to *move*) will give him a very powerful urge to walk. Once he starts, there's no stopping him, and he will be constantly on the go.

TODDLE-TUNE ROCKER
Little Tikes

ACTION PUSH TOYS

When the toddler is a little more steady on his feet he will enjoy action push toys like that perennial favorite, the Fisher-Price *Corn Popper*, and any of a multitude of similar toys. These playthings combine a sound-and-action device at the end of a long handle, controlled by the child as he pushes.

• FISHER-PRICE also makes a *Rattle Ball* push toy which is filled with multi-colord beads, and the company offers *Melody Push Chime*.

• BRIMA's *Roller Walker* is noisy and colorful when your toddler pushes it and makes its clackers turn.

• KIDDICRAFT makes two push toys that are filled with personality—*Push Along Clown* with his big floppy feet and his jaunty red bow tie performs as he moves. He chuckles and his head bobs up and down—quite a happy-go-lucky fellow! The *Push Along Duck* waddles as he walks. Both toys are painted in bold primary colors.

Push toys stimulate walking, and the sound effects captivate your toddler and add great pleasure to the play. The toddler loves to play "chase me" games. He entices the parent to come after him. In chasing his push toy, he has his own game, giggling and squeaking as he goes.

Toddlers also enjoy pushing their own carriages or strollers. Incidentally, pull toys won't be used for another few months until walking is firmly established. These are discussed in the next chapter.

INDOOR GYMS

As soon as your child can walk, you may want to consider an indoor slide and climbers. Movement, especially gross motor movement, is all-important to the child at this time. Just imagine the dimension that walking has added to his life. He is truly independent. As your toddler grows, the need for physical play also grows. He must be on the go constantly—or so it seems to you.

There are two toddler gyms designed for the child of this age and ability. They are safe and they are a perfect challenge for all of that energy.

• CHILDCRAFT features a *Toddler's Gym* that is, basically, a three-step ladder, a platform with handrail and a 36"-long slide. Under the platform is a crawl-through space that can be used as a tunnel or hideaway. These gyms encourage the climbing, sliding, crawling and hiding so enjoyed by little children.

• LITTLE TIKES' *Playslide* also has an easy-to-climb, wide-based ladder with a few steps. It has a molded-grip handle for the child to hold while he climbs to the top of the gym. The slide is gently sloped. This indoor gym folds for easy storage.

PLAYSLIDE
Little Tikes

Although this may be expensive equipment, it will interest a child all through the preschool years and will probably give more play hours per dollar invested than any other item except wooden kindergarten blocks.

FEEDING GAMES

During this period of his general drive toward independence, your baby will inevitably try feeding himself at some point. Of course he doesn't yet have the eye-hand coordination or the control over his wrist to be able to accomplish this without a great deal of spilling and upsetting. You may feel that feeding him yourself is preferable to cleaning up after him, but remember that he needs to try to feed himself as a necessary part of self-assertion. You can help him by providing appropriate eating implements and as many finger foods as possible. The drive to be independent is very real when it comes to eating. He will want to feed himself long before he has mastered the art of handling a fork or a spoon—or fine table manners.

He shows his determination to take over when he tries to grab the cup or spoon that you are feeding him with. Before long he will vigorously attempt to push your hand away. Everything spills before it can reach his mouth. The toddler loves to mess about and play with his food. In this way he will discover all kinds of textures—gooey, soft, hard, liquid, solid, temperatures and taste sensations.

The right utensils will help the child feed himself. The best kind of spoon has a short, straight, broad handle. The child can then grasp it easily with his whole fist. It should have a wide mouth and be shallow so that he is able to put it into his mouth sideways. At this age, he cannot crook his wrist sufficiently to eat comfortably with a conventional spoon.

The fork should also have a straight, broad handle about as long as the width of a child's fist. The point should be blunt. His plate and bowl should have sides so that a baby can push against it with his fork or spoon.

Learning to drink from a cup will be easier for your child than mastering the spoon and fork. A training cup, which is weighted, is designed to allow your baby to teach himself how to drink.

THE FIRST YEARS has designed a cup that is just right for your baby's hands. The shape of the cup makes it self-righting, and the fact it does not have a heavily weighted bottom makes it easier for a young child to handle. It comes with two handles and three screw-on lids that can't pop off. You will want to start him off by using the lid with the sucking-drinking spout. When he becomes accustomed to holding and lifting the cup, switch to the lid with the hole. After he has gained techniques and confidence, you can try it without the lids.

Encourage your baby's self-feeding by giving him finger foods. Hamburger cut into small pieces, bread spread with cream cheese or jam, pieces of boiled potato, peas, carrots, slices of bananas, slices of peeled apples are all foods he can pick up and nibble on by himself. Make the setting as attractive as possible. Remember, however, that his need to explore and move about will not allow him to sit still for a long time.

Color of food, and consistency are things to think about when putting the menu together. Food that sticks together is easier to handle than soup or runny foods. He likes bland flavors better than sharp tastes. And above all children like variety—something that's raw, then something that's crisp, then something that's chewy.

Take this time to socialize with your child and make eating a pleasant experience. During the next few years you will be introducing him to a number of new foods.

CONTAINER, NESTING AND PILING TOYS

The child of one-year-plus will have more diverse interests and more sophisticated tastes than ever before. He still likes container toys and especially enjoys putting smaller objects into larger ones and then dumping them out. Several smaller objects will amuse him more than one large one, and he will entertain himself at length in the continuous cycle of fill-and-dump activity: picking objects up one by one, dropping them, picking them up again, putting them into receptacles and dumping them. This seemingly random activity is actually a rudimentary form of counting—his first lesson in arithmetic.

A good dumping and filling toy can be easily made at home. Cut a large round hole in the cover of an oatmeal box or a shoe box and show your baby how to drop blocks or empty thread spools through the hole, then how to take off the lid and dump out the contents. This play will fascinate your baby and he will repeat the cycle over and over with great enjoyment.

Your baby's eye-hand coordination continues to improve, and he is able to place objects *where* he wants and, more importantly, release them *when* he wants with increasing precision. If you have not already purchased the classic peg with graduated discs, get him one now.

The *Discovery Ball* by AMBI, a Dutch import, is an interesting take-apart/put-together toy that will further encourage the development of his sense of size. This is a variation of the simple stacking pyramid and appeals to your baby's interest in multiple objects and his love of piling objects one on top of another. The discs can be assembled on the spindle in a variety of ways and a steel ball inside the center peg makes the completed ball roll when pushed. Size comparisons must be made by the child because if a part is misplaced, the smaller piece disappears into the larger.

With these toys and a variety of household objects, your baby is discovering exactly what "size" means. He is discovering that size is relative—that "big" or "little" is meaningless until the object is compared to another object of a different size.

The child must make size comparisons—big, bigger, biggest and small, smaller, smallest. All such stacking toys, introduced earlier as rings dropped over a center pole and later as more complicated shapes, relate to future learning, especially in reading and numbers.

You will want to continue to have a variety of container, nesting and piling toys for your baby to work with at this stage. In addition to the graduated round nesting cups you have probably already given him, your child will be ready for a variety of other shapes in this type of toy.

• CHILD GUIDANCE's *Learning Tower* is now a classic. There are twelve soft cups which stack on top of each other. It comes in four different colors so that your child can build a tower of three cups of each color. Side by side, these towers can illustrate small, middle-sized, large or big, bigger, biggest.

• DISCOVERY TOY's *Kitty In The Kegs* is a toy within a nesting and stacking toy. Five kegs are nested in one larger keg. Kitty is found in the smallest keg. Once taken apart, the colorful kegs can be stacked according to size.

The toddler at this age can build a tower of three items, so you may have to guide him in adding another one or two stories.

He likes to hold things and put them into something. Since he is developing finer eye-hand coordination, he can place an object where he wants with a fair amount of accuracy. He can also pick up and let go with either hand. Remember, he is beginning to do pre-counting exercises. As he picks up and puts down one item after another, he is doing a rudimentary kind of counting.

TOYS TO GROW ON's *Stack-A-Ball* will introduce the toddler to differences in numbers. The child sorts and stacks 15 hardwood balls on five wooden dowels of varying heights. Beginning with a blue ball, he places just one on the first, short dowel. Then two green on the next, followed by three yellow, four orange and, finally, five red balls—all stacked in a row. At first, he will approach the game from the simplest point of view.

Since he loves playing games, take the opportunity to use the toy to play with him. Ask him to put one ball on a dowel identifying the color as you do so. Then you place one on in a different color. As he practices fitting and piling, he will have a chance to join in the give and

STACK 'N STORE NESTING CUBES
Little Tikes

take of language. Talk to him about color and numbers while you are playing. His attention span may still be short. If he is restless and wants to leave the toy, you can come back to it later.

Make sure that he learns how to drop the ball over the dowel with ease before you begin more complicated play. Eventually, he will be able to mix and match colors and place all five on the final dowel all by himself.

• JOHNSON & JOHNSON's *Puzzle Post* is an intriguing variation on this theme. It is a shape sorting, nesting and stacking toy. All the shapes fit, one within the other, over a removable center post. They can be placed in any order. These simple shapes—circles, squares, triangles will help your child learn basic forms. Each shape has broad sides so that your toddler can also build a tall tower. The circular shapes can be rolled about. All are in bold primary colors.

PUZZLE POST
Johnson & Johnson

• LITTLE TIKES offers *Stack 'N Store Nesting Cubes*—an atractive set of cubes in red, yellow, blue, green and orange, ranging in size from very large to hand-sized cubes. Each cube is illustrated with brightly colored graphics. The cubes fit inside one another or stack to build a tower 20 inches high.

The same company has designed a unique combination of stacking, nesting and shape recognition in *Tubby Tug Tug*. The base is a white boat with smiling faces at each porthole. Baby can fit two peg sailors and a nautical flag into the boat. This amphibious tug can be used on land or in water.

HAMMERING TOYS

At approximately fourteen months, your baby will be ready for a hammering toy. This toy is essentially a group of pegs in a frame. There are many kinds of pounding benches available. In some versions, the pegs are actually knocked out of the frame. But, this could prove unsatisfactory since the pegs are likely to be scattered and lost.

• PLAYSKOOL's *Cobbler's Bench* is representative of a very practical version. The toddler pounds upon pegs which are placed in holes on the outline of the sole of a shoe. As he bangs these pegs into place he is "fixing" the shoe. The bench, mallet and six colorful pegs are made of wood.

• PLAYSKOOL's *Flip Around Pounder* is a different version of the pounding bench. In this design, four beads are strung on an arch. When the child hits the lever with the mallet, one of the beads flips over the arch. Next to the arch is a red wheel which makes a ratchet sound when one of the spokes is hit with the mallet.

• BRIO's *Hammer the Beads* bench is one of the best. The imaginative toy features four brightly colored balls which are hammered through

COBBLER'S BENCH
Playskool

holes in the top. They disappear into a red and yellow box and reappear through a hole in the bottom, ready to be replaced on top and hammered down again.

Note the continuous-action feature of these hammering toys. The completion of the action is also the preparation for a repetition of the action. The child is tempted into continuing the activity and, in a subtle way, is being encouraged to lengthen his span of attention.

BLOCKS

For balancing and stacking, your baby will still enjoy the soft blocks from his creeping days, but he can also begin to use wooden blocks. The most common blocks are the two-inch wooden cubes and these are widely available.

Blocks give the child experiences in manipulating various sizes and shapes, thereby increasing manual dexterity. As he tries to build with his blocks, he is beginning his relationship with problem solving. This activity helps prepare him to handle school problems later on, especially in mathematics.

A beginner set of polished hardwood blocks offering three or four different geometric shapes will provide your baby with imaginative play well into the nursery years. Begin with a basic set of blocks and keep adding to them as he grows in his ability to build towers, bridges, houses or whatever his creativity urges him to build.

This is a wonderful time for parent and child to play and build together. Let him start. Ask him what he is building. As he adds another block, another shape, talk to him about the sizes and colors. Talk to him about his creation. At this stage he may require your help. Soon he will become the architect of a design of the future.

• PLAYSKOOL makes a variety of blocks in natural hardwood, in colored wood, and they make kindergarten wood blocks. The first two sets of between 35 to 49 blocks come in a number of geometric shapes— squares, oblongs, diagonals, triangles, pillars, and half columns. The kindergarten set adds a roman arch and a half circle. All have rounded corners and edges.

• F.A.O. SCHWARZ offers a set of colorful and graphic nested picture blocks. Some show old-fashioned childhood scenes; others are illustrated with ABCs and numbers.

• FISHER-PRICE's *Creative Blocks* are also a classic toy. The set contains 12 pieces in various shapes in bright, primary colors.

Soon after your child's first birthday, he will begin to show an elemental interest in music, art and language. He will very much enjoy simple, rhythmically accented sounds and will respond to music with great delight. You might give him his very own music box, either the crank-handle version or the kind wound with a key. If you have the crank-handle type, you may find that your baby will make efforts to crank it himself. You can help him by holding your hand over his to make him familiar with the turning hand action. There is a wide range in the quality of music boxes, from the tinny, hurdy-gurdy type to the exquisite (and costly) ones imported from Switzerland. However, you will want an inexpensive one for your toddler unless you keep it well out of his reach.

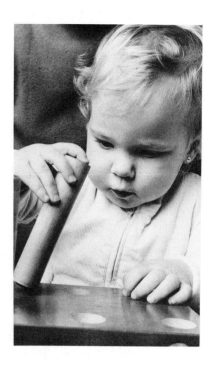

This is the time when he will especially enjoy nursery rhymes and jingles. You can read rhymes from such books as *The New Golden Song Book* (Western Publishing). Your baby's command of language is increasing all the time, and he already is associating more and more words with their meanings. By the time he is fifteen months old, his vocabulary will probably include five or six real words, and he will understand much of what you say to him. If you ask him to give you something, the chances are he will know what you mean, whether or not he complies.

PICTURE BOOKS

Continue to introduce him to the lovely world of picture books. One of his favorite pastimes will be sitting in your lap and having you read to him, and he will do his very best to try to help you turn the pages. Expect him to grasp several at once at first. The concept of turning one page at a time is a new one for him, and he does not have the dexterity to do it.

Picture books are important because the association between pictures and the names of the objects they represent reinforces, clarifies and expands the learning he has already picked up. Books at this stage are used not so much for reading as for vocabulary-building and for labeling objects with their proper names. You may notice a curious thing when you first introduce picture books—your baby may not recognize an object on the page that he knows very well in reality. For instance, he may look intently at a picture of a shoe and show no indication of having seen it before. Be assured that this is a common occurrence indicating that his visual perception is not yet developed sufficiently for him to associate the two-dimensional representation with the three-dimensional reality. Conversely, although he can identify perfectly well the cow in his picture book, he may not recognize a live cow when he first sees one. Understanding these things, you will see the importance of selecting picture books which contain illustrations of both familiar and unfamiliar objects.

• Among the best first books are the ones designed by DICK BRUNA. His books are sold in better bookstores. The Dick Bruna books have heavy, plastic-coated cardboard pages, each showing a single brightly colored picture. Children prefer bright colors, even if they seem garish to you; their vision does not yet respond to gentle, pastel hues.

Also look for the many picture books of baby animals, farm animals and zoo animals, particularly the ones which have color photographs mounted on heavy cardboard pages. These are popular with children at this age and all through the preschool years.

• PRICE/STERN/SLOAN's Peter Curry series of wonderful and brightly illustrated books will excite any young child. *ABCs, Colors, Shapes,* and *Numbers* will delight your toddler until he can read them by himself. The rhymes on each page pose questions you can ask your child.

> Can you see the triangle?
> Where is something square?
> How many circles can you find?
> Can you name some more shapes?

This is advanced reading for your child. But, since he is now playing with geometric blocks, you can help him learn to match the shape of the blocks in his hand to the one shown in the book. The colors he will be seeing in his collection of toys will appear on each lovely page of the book.

As he develops in understanding letters and number concepts, he will surely enjoy pointing to the ABCs and the 1's, 2's and 3's graphically illustrated in this series of books.

• SIMON & SCHUSTER's *The Little Simon Learner* books are a lovely set of first readers that encourage young children to speak. The publishers write, "One of the very first things that your child does when starting to talk is to name objects that are seen and used everyday." This series of First Words books, Time to Talk books and Look And Say books features all the familiar objects the toddler is coming in contact with all the time.

The baby has spent his first year in a pre-language state, listening most of the time and then babbling in response to your words. Now he will spend his time in a pre-speech state, developing a readiness to talk. Your child begins to recognize that certain sounds stand for certain objects.

By his twelfth month he can understand some words. "Show me the cup," Dad may ask. The child will look toward or point to the cup. By the time he is fifteen months old, he is paying attention to sounds coming from another room or outside the home. These are sounds he may have ignored before.

Some children at this age can identify parts of their bodies. However, they will still need your guidance and gestures to help understand what you are saying. Say "nose" and he will point to his nose; say "mouth" and he will touch his mouth.

A child's first words are most often words of command or words of recognition. They will not be pronounced perfectly. "Goggie" may mean dog. But, it may also mean a cat, a stuffed toy animal or a horse. Terms are general now. You can help him understand the many differences as you name individually each object he shows you.

Two other types of vocalization appear in the second year: jargon and echolalia.

Jargon is a stream of unintelligable jabber which appears between the 12th and 15th month. He is practicing fluency. He is no longer just playing with sounds, but is jabbering with a purpose. He is talking to his toys, to you, to anyone who will listen.

Later as he reaches his 18th month, he begins to parrot the speach he hears (echolalia). He usually does this without thinking:

Mother says, "Do you want some milk?"

He answers, "want some milk?"

And so it will continue throughout the day. He likes to play with his voice when he is alone, usually at the end of the day. You will hear him playing with repeated syllables or making the "s" sounds.

You can make a very personalized picture book for your child by cutting out photographs and illustrations from old magazines or mail order catalogs and pasting them on cardboard. Five inches by eight inches is a good page size for the baby to hold and focus on. Use only one picture to a page. You can make them into a book by punching holes near the edge of the sheets, top and bottom, and tying a cord through the holes.

The classic participation book beloved by toddlers is Dorothy Kunhardt's *Pat the Bunny* (WESTERN PUBLISHING). The child feels a soft cotton bunny, looks at himself in a shiny foil mirror, smells the flowers on a scented page, feels Daddy's scratchy sandpaper beard, etc. Western Publishing has a charming set of scent books. In *Bunny Follows His Nose*, baby scratches the strawberry and smells the scent; when he rubs the chocolate, chocolate fills the air. Other books are about the scents of Christmas, the woods and a birthday party.

The traditonal nursery rhymes and Mother Goose verses are fun to read with your child. *The Baby's Lap Book* by Kay Chorao Dutton contains soft drawings in pretty pastel colors of favorite nursery rhymes and nursery games.

There are so many books available we suggest you browse through your favorite children's book store or the local library. In these outlets a sales clerk or the librarian will be a valuable source of information and assistance. It is important to try to select the best books for this age group. Your child and you will appreciate the fact that the quality of the subject matter, art work or photos and the whole approach in writing are for the young child. Quality books keep growing with the child, the contents taking on new meaning each time the child reads them.

An excellent children's bookstore which carries a full collection of books for children of all ages is Eeyore's in New York City. You can get a catalog by writing to Eeyore's at 1066 Madison Avenue, New York, N.Y. 10028.

Your child has now reached a level in his development that surely seemed impossible a short time ago. He can walk by himself and is beginning to talk. He can name a few familiar objects, and he is starting to engage in more complicated projects. He's experimenting with feeding himself, cooperating a bit in dressing and becoming increasingly sociable. Certainly, he is constantly on the move. It must seem strange that such a short time ago your baby needed you every minute, and now he is showing such signs of independence.

When he feels comfortable and secure, he will move away from you to another room. But soon he uses up that feeling, the need to be reassured gains the upper hand, and he comes rushing back for a hug or merely to make certain you're still there. This pattern of venturing off and then touching base again is one which is repeated in various forms over and over again throughout childhood.

You can help encourage his independence by letting him out of his carriage whenever he wants to walk, by lifting him out of the playpen when he is tired of it and by giving him plenty of opportunities to get used to strangers, both adults and children. But don't push him to approach or play with strangers. You cannot force his independence by leaving him alone with unfamiliar people before he is ready for it.

In short, give him as much freedom as he wants to explore his world, but make sure he knows you are always *there* in the background lending your support. You'll be spending extra time watching him to see that he doesn't get into dangerous situations, and you will spend lots of extra effort cleaning up after him. But, you will be more than repaid by the difference in his development. You wouldn't for all the world stifle his healthy, natural curiosity when you realize that this is the way he learns at the age of one-year-plus.

Fifteen to Eighteen Months
"I'll Do It Myself"

Toddlerhood truly emerges and surges during the next few months. This stage of childhood continues until he is 2½ years old and the preschool period begins. Child researchers claim that for physical development, self-esteem, learning and autonomy, toddlerhood is a critical period. Being a toddler has been compared to being an adolescent. The toddler is hovering between babyhood and childhood, looking for ways in which to try out his new independence. Since most of the basic developmental milestones have been reached, the toddler is free and confident to set out under his own steam.

At fifteen months, the toddler continues to make wonderful discoveries of self. He is aware of himself, as distinguished from being aware of others around him. As a result, he wants to "do it myself" more than ever. And, he has added, "Now!" to this desire. As Dr. Alvin Eden writes in *Positive Parenting*, "If you think you were tired before, during the nine to twelve months stage, the real fun is only beginning."

The period between the ages of one and two years is a time of very rapid motor, language and emotional development as well as continuing physical growth. At some point along the way, you will realize that you no longer have a baby in the family. Your child has become a separate, independent individual with a mind of his own—he has become a child. The short span of time between fifteen months and a year-and-a-half is an important transitional period from the total dependence of babyhood to the relative independence of the two-year-old.

These may be trying times for your child. He will occasionally show signs of frustration and anger when he is overwhelmed by the difficulties of coordinating new skills. He has, according to Dr. Gesell, "an extraordinary diversity of behavior patterns to coordinate and consolidate." He will undoubtedly be somewhat difficult to deal with, and will tend to be negative and to resist you. Try to remember that this is a necessary stage in his becoming a separate individual in control of himself.

Part of his difficulty is caused by the fact that so many new abilities are developing all at once. His foremost achievement, of course, is *verticality*—he can now stand up without help and can walk alone. This new mobility marks the beginning of a period of ceaseless activity when he will be into everything.

New manipulative skills are also coming into play, and his command of language is increasing every day. His playthings for this period will need to challenge all of these growing powers.

The physical energy of the fifteen- to eighteen-month-old is tremendous, and he will need lots of outlets for it. He'll be lugging, tugging, pulling, pushing, dragging, dumping, taking things from place to place, abandoning them, resuming the activity in a different manner and never stopping for a minute. This energetic behavior is very self-involved, and he won't be interested in playmates yet. He and his friends will play near each other, but not together, with each absorbed in his own separate activity.

At times, your child may seem wildly mercurial and even frantic, but still he performs certain tasks with a sense of decisiveness and finality. *Here* and *now* are important to him. He likes *endings* as well as *beginnings* in his growing understanding of the concept that things stop as well as start. Some of his work is done with a definite feeling of completion. "There, I've finished," he almost seems to say as he hands you his empty milk cup, and if you don't accept it right away, it may end up on the floor. He's not being contrary; he's just telling you he's done with it.

SAND, MUD AND WATER

To accompany all this bustling energy, his primary need is for play equipment to develop his big muscles. If you do not yet have the sort of indoor gym described in the previous chapter, you may want to get one now or improvise a substitute. You can use boxes or discarded furniture to create your own gym and satisfy your toddler's urge to climb. A wide board or a table leaf supported at either end by blocks or thick phone books (if you live in a big city) makes a good climbing bridge.

In addition to climbing, the other new large-muscle activity your child enjoys now is his newborn ability to throw. The toddler is making his first tentative efforts at this skill, which will have improved greatly by the time he is eighteen months old. Even now he can enjoy a continuous-action game of throwing his ball and dashing after it. Or you can introduce him to the fun of a simple game of catch with a large rubber ball. At the beginning, though, remember it will take a while for the baby to master the intricacies of time and space so that he can have his hands at the right place at the right time to catch the ball.

Your toddler is moving around at such a nonstop pace that you may often wonder if there isn't something that will lure him into sitting still for a while. Yes, there is. In fact, there are three things—all free, or nearly so—that every child loves and needs: sand, mud and water. Prepare for several years of gritty floors and extra laundry, because these natural playthings that have been enjoyed since prehistoric times are among the most important for every child's development.

Sand, mud and water encourage freedom and inventiveness. They satisfy the child's need to be messy. He is discouraged from smearing his food or his soiled diapers, but it is all right for him to do what he wants with these substances. The joy of feeling free-flowing sand, squishy mud and splashy water are exhilarating to the child who still receives so many sensations through his fingers.

A sand area should be big enough for the child to sit in. It doesn't necessarily have to be a sand box, because all of the sand won't stay inside it anyway. The only sand toys necessary now are a big sturdy wooden or metal spoon for digging and a cup or small pail. Filling the cup and pouring out the sand, a version of fill-and-dump activity that has occupied him for some time, will be his main interest now. Later you can add a sifter, a funnel and sand-shaping tools, but for now, keep it simple. When he's playing in the dirt or mud, a spoon alone will be sufficient.

If you are a city-dweller, find the sand pile in your park or provide a "sand tray" at home. A shallow box with a few inches of sand and a few cups will keep him interested for quite a while.

Ideally, water play should take place in a plastic wading pool outdoors in summer, but you can also easily provide it all year around. Give your toddler a chance to play in the water while he is having his bath, or let him play in the dry tub with a pan of lukewarm water. In this way there will be less mopping up to do than when he plays with water at the sink. Early water toys can include a sponge, a ball, a squeeze bottle, a cup, empty spools, corks. Later additions might be a small rubber doll to bathe, a rubber-bulbed meat baster and a second cup so the water can be poured back and forth between the two. Have a variety of things available, but give him only a few things at one time.

SPLASH & STACK BLUEBIRD
Fisher-Price Toys

Several water toys that were introduced to the baby during the past few months will continue to delight now.

• JOHNSON & JOHNSON's *Balls In A Bowl* is a great bath toy. The smaller balls, containing moving objects that rotate, rattle and twirl, float about in the bath. The large yellow ball, the container for the three small balls, can be filled with water and emptied.

• FISHER-PRICE's *Splash and Stack Bluebird* comes apart for pouring and straining. The baby bird within the large Bluebird squirts and squeaks.

• KIDDICRAFT's three *Red, White and Blue Ducks* can be invited to join the traditional Yellow Duck in the bath. Each colorful duck features a tail spout for pouring out water or sand, and all three may be linked together head to tail. They are stackable.

• KIDDICRAFT's *Water-Mate Duck* is the most charming of all the yellow duckies. He floats within a glass ball which, in turn, floats in the bath. This duck remains upright however the ball is rolled or floated.

• CHILD GUIDANCE's set of familiar *Sesame Street Spinning Pals* are fun to watch. Each character spins when the ball is rolled. Ernie, the Cookie Monster and Big Bird are contained within a clear ball small enough for the child to grasp easily.

• LITTLE TIKES offers two interesting, take-apart boats—*Tubby Tug Tug*, described in previous chapters, and *Tub 'N Barge Set* which includes a sailor, a red barge and a blue and white tugboat.

• JOHNSON & JOHNSON's *Shipshape Village* is a more intricate and versatile water toy. This brightly colored set can be used in the bath, in the sandbox or on the floor. The pieces fit together in a variety of ways. The fisherman and sea captain fit in the boat or can be hidden under a house for disappearing games. The red boat snugly fits into the green harbor. The houses make super scoops for water play. They are made of soft vinyl so that they can be chewed.

• BERCHET has designed a beautifully colored *Fish Rattle* that is an unusual water toy. The red ball within the fish's tummy spins as water flows in and out. The gracefully carved fin is shaped so baby can grab it and propel the fish along.

Berchet also makes *Bath Harbor* which combines a series of water play features. The paddle wheel turns when water is poured over it; a boat nozzle squirts water; the fish cup lifts out for pouring; the harbor gate opens up; and a winch pulls the tug back into the harbor with an easy turn of the crank. The colors (bright red, yellow and dark blue) are wonderful to look at. All of this activity attaches to side of tub.

• FISHER-PRICE's *Bath Activity Center* contains all sorts of intriguing devices to help baby experience cause and effect. A cup lifts out for pouring; a whale spouts water; dolphins spin and the bright blue octopus pops out from a hiding place.

All children love to play with water. Bath time is a perfect time to spend playing with your child since it is very important *never* to leave a child alone when he is in the bath or playing near water. Show him how water flows from one container to another. Make the fish or boat plow through the water. He will be amazed to see the ball pop to the top and float after your push it to the bottom of the tub.

• LITTLE TIKES offers the *Marina Sandbox* play center for water and sand play—if you have the room. The red sandbox features a specially designed roadway for vehicles that can be driven around the perimeter, and the cover has a waterway for sailing boats around a center island that is linked to the mainland by yellow bridges. Cleverly designed, the Marina Sandbox measures 33 inches square by 6¼ inches high.

PULL TOYS

Now that your child can walk well, he will really enjoy pull toys. There is an infinite variety to choose from. Make sure the one your choose is not too heavy or cumbersome for him to control with ease— remember, he's still a toddler. It is also helpful if these toys make some kind of sound to reassure your child that they are still there without his looking around to check.

• BRIO makes the best collection of pull-along toys. They are colorful, sturdy (made of wood) and frequently contain more than one activity. Their *Clown Wagon* holds a clown that whirls his arms and rings chimes on the wagon as he is pulled along. Three small rings can be stacked onto a dowel fitted on the front of the wagon.

Oscar Worm shyly slinks along; the ball perched on the tip of the Seal's nose rolls around when he is pulled.

There are so many delightful Brio characters to take for a walk that you may want to write for a catalog or take your child on a shopping trip so that he can choose his favorite.

Several pull-along toys come in unconventional shapes. For instance, there are long, snake-like toys sporting numerous wheels which make them 'slither' behind the toddler.

• TOYS TO GROW ON has a *Wheely Pull Toy* that is a collection of multi-colored wheels attached to a center wooden core. This flexible pull-along toy in six vibrant colors can be stretched out or piled into a pyramid shape. You can find Wheely in the toymaker's catalog.

• WALTER WOOD TOYS presents *Bim Bim*, a two-in-one pull toy. Three gaily decorated bell rattles sit along the center core which is surrounded by eight multi-colored wooden wheels. The rattles can be taken off and played with individually. This company also has a colorful collection of pull-along creatures. *Hippopotamus* happily carries a "clicking" bird on his back. The *Duck Chain* is a family of three ducks. The *Airplane* has wings that move up and down while the propeller spins when this toy is pulled across the floor.

• KIDDICRAFT's red, blue and yellow *Clatterpillar* smiles shyly as he wobbles and clatters along on his ten legs.

• KOUVALIAS OF ATHENS has created a beautiful series of wooden pull toys in shiny primary colors and imaginative forms. There are several different dogs and ducks, there is a swan with an egg, and outer-space-type figures that jiggle about as they move. Their *Ferris Wheel*, fashioned of gently waving balls on springs, makes a tinkling sound as it strike the bell. Another toy is a creation of little mushrooms that revolve and strike a bell as the toy is pulled. The Kouvalias toys are worth seeking out in specialty toy stores or department stores.

• FISHER-PRICE has the most appealing collection of pull toys made of a variety of materials. *Snoopy Dog* has been following toddlers around for almost fifty years—a traditional first pet. Their airplane with moving propellers is great fun. Once again, there are so many interesting figures and characters your child will want to pick out his favorite friend.

• BRIMA makes several lovely looking wooden animals to pull along. *Hop-A-Long Bunny* is a bright red with the sort of brilliant gloss finish that gives Brima toys their superb look. The Bunny hops perkily along when pulled.

• AMBI's *Play Jet* offers the toddler several play activities. The Jet makes a gentle noise when pulled or pushed along. Inside, four peg people sit patiently in the plane until it is time to get off. The tail wing is also removeable and makes a whistling jet sound when blown.

Many pull toys are ornamented with miniature figures that are activated by mechanical devices. The little figures may dance, tumble, clap or play musical instrument in an ingenious way. These toys should be considered novelties. They have great amusement value for a short time at the expense of durability; their delicate parts break easily; their mechanisms may go out of order. However, many of these toys *are* amusing and attractive, and if you are willing to spend the money, some of the most charming are sold through F.A.O. Schwarz.

You can make your own pull toy by tying lightweight, unbreakable, sound-making objects onto a cord or a long work-shoe lace. Knot the objects a few inches apart, and attach the end that the child will hold to a large wooden bead. Several milk cartons or shoe boxes will make a great train; metal jar caps (with holes punched through) can be strung

LITTLE SNOOPY
Fisher-Price Toys

with thread spools to make a caterpillar pull toy. Old bracelets, rattles and most kitchen utensils can be a part of your design.

• LITTLE TIKES' *Wagon 'N Friends* is a combination of four bright-eyed animals and pull along wagon. The orange giraffe, yellow duck, blue elephant and green puppy on wheels all fit into the wagon. They can be arranged peering over the edge waiting for the ride to start or the animals can all be linked together in a procession.

• JOHNSON & JOHNSON's *Rhythm Rollers* is a challenging pull toy with a wide range of play possibilities. The bright red truck carries a musical cargo of cylinders, each decorated differently, and it makes a clack, rattle and jingle sound if it is pulled or handled.

There are small pull wagons filled with wooden blocks that are available almost everywhere. The wagons are usually wood, and the brightly colored blocks in plain or decorated designs or alphabet letters come in a variety of shapes. The play value of this simple, combination toy is unreal. The toddler can fill and dump, pull and push, build and tear down, and the wagon can be a doll's bed for years. Its function will change again and again as the child's imagination grows and his physical skills develop. The best are made by: PLAYSKOOL, FISHER-PRICE, BRIO and T.C. TIMBER. All are loaded with well-made hardwood blocks that are easy for the young child to handle. The designs on the blocks will stimulate imaginative play and verbal interaction.

BLOCKS

Blocks will continue to play an increasingly important role in the child's life. Your child begins by holding one block; then he holds one in each hand; then he places one on top of another. Now that he is nearly eighteen months he may be able to stack three or four blocks successfully. But don't expect him to spend his whole time stacking—he will pound them together to hear their sound and will carry them around the room with him as he rushes from one activity to another.

Dr. Arnold Gesell, founder of the Yale University Clinic of Child Development, wrote, "It is highly significant from the point of view of human development that the child's own initiative, his own behavior drive produces this block building behavior."

Now that the toddler wants to handle everything he sees, to understand what is happening, blocks are the perfect plaything to help in his discoveries. Since he has learned to walk and stand upright, his hands are free to hold any number of interesting things. With a set of blocks he can learn about stacking, balancing, shapes and sizes. With your help he can build a variety of items—a bridge, a small house, a fence, Dadda's office, a four-story tower. Blocks put end to end make a boat or train or a truck or whatever he sees as being horizontal.

BASIC BLOCK SET
DUPLO

For the creative and imaginative skills they foster, blocks are worth any other ten toys to the child of this age and on beyond to his preschool years.

MANIPULATIVE TOYS

You can take advantage of your child's increased interest in using his hands—give him toys that will help him exercise and practice manipulative skills. He needs toys that use the small muscles, that allow him to grasp and release, take apart and put together, put into and dump out of. You will notice how much his manual dexterity has increased. He can now pick up things and put them down when and where he wants to. He does much of his learning through his hands and all of his sensory apparatus.

There are several manipulative toys which not only offer the toddler a chance to practice these skills but also are excellent in stimulating imaginative play.

• LEGO's DUPLO Block system gives the toddler a chance to handle smaller, put-together block pieces in bright colors to create his own playthings. This building-block system is sized just right for the toddler—not too small, and the sets have a limited number of pieces so that he can finish an item in a few steps. Sets in the Playville series are made up of three to seven pieces placed in individual carrying cases. The *Pony Trailer* features a cowboy who fits into a yellow jeep which pulls a trailer for his horse. *Sports Car, Fire Truck* and *Tub Boat* and *Car* are all fun to create.

Two fantasy sets are somewhat more complex (21 – 29 pieces). There is a *Barnyard* with farm animals; a *Windmill*, which has to be made; a *Cowboy* and *Fence*; and a *Nursery School* with teacher, school children, blackboard, shelf and clock. He will be completely absorbed working with these sets and will get satisfaction out of completing an item. He may require your help with some of the pieces and figures. One reward will be discussing the whole thing with you when he has finished.

• PLAYSKOOL's *Star Links* come in several bright, lovely colors. Each star-shaped piece with its six knobby spokes locks to the next with a snap. They can be pulled apart with ease. This design allows the child to build in all directions.

STAR LINKS
Playskool

Wonder Blocks are large interlocking blocks made to fit a small hand. These multi-colored blocks are designed for building a tall tower that will not fall over. They can be interlocked in staggered fashion to form a curving or sepentine wall. Begin with simple patterns at this age, and, literally, build to more complex figures.

• CHILD GUIDANCE presents *Nuts 'N Bolts*, a more difficult toy in this same category. Twenty nuts and bolts are screwed together by color and size.

All of the sorting and the other problem-solving aspects of these toys will help the toddler build a foundation for mathematical thinking. While he is playing, he will be learning about the relationships between objects.

Talk to him about the colors and shapes he is handling. Ask him about what he has made, and talk to him about the particular features of each object. When you are looking at the barnyard animals in the Duplo play scenes, for instance, say "This is a horse. The horse says 'neigh.'" Or, "Here is the cowboy who is taking care of his animals." Then, have him point out the cowboy to you.

• BRIO has some toys suitable for the child of nearly eighteen months that are deserving of mention. Gearboards, trays with a pattern of small spindles holding removable gears that mesh and turn, are interesting to a baby of this age.

COG LABYRINTH
BRIO

Remember, your child's attention span is still short, so he will lose interest in a toy or a project after a while, leave it, and then come back. Much of the time he will be dashing about testing his new ambulatory skills, but this exuberant motion will be punctuated by quiet intervals when he will actually sit down in one spot and concentrate on one thing. At this stage of his development, he has a keen interest in objects with several parts.

At a year and a half, the child is becoming increasingly fascinated by adult activities and will delight in imitating them. He will love to follow you around with his toy dust mop or broom, or pretend that he is cooking with pots and pans. He may use his toy pans or some of your real ones. If you are like every other mother we know, you spend a certain amount of time on the telephone, so the child would particularly enjoy his very own little wood or plastic telephone to use.

He is beginning to project himself into the world outside and is not nearly so closely identified with his mother as he has been. He wants to be able to do what you do, however, so always encourage him to take part in the daily activites of the family.

Now your child will probably have a vocabulary of ten or so words. He will respond to some words and short phrases. He begins to call himself by name. He continues to babble on contentedly in a kind of jargon known only to himself and perhaps to another child at home. However, he will be listening carefully, picking up every signal, so you will want to talk to him a great deal. We suggest you *do not* use baby talk!

Let him know right away how to pronounce words correctly. Identify objects with their proper names. Encourage him to repeat what you say as you name objects, colors, foods, etc., to him. All children start out by mispronouncing most of the words they learn, but, as in everything he will be doing, practice makes perfect and corrective feedback is enormously important.

The most important technique of language development is repetition—he learns by saying things (in his fashion) again and again. In the next few months he will improve very quickly, and you will soon be bombarded with endless demands for the names of everything he sees. This may be tiresome and exasperating to you, but it is an extremely vital process in your child's learning.

READ-ALOUD BOOKS

By eighteen months, your child will be pointing to objects in his books and naming them, and he will be a little more adroit at helping you turn the pages. He will enjoy the rhythms and repetitions of nursery rhymes. There probably aren't enough shelves in the world to hold all of the available books of nursery rhymes, but we will suggest a few good titles. Western Publishing has *Best Mother Goose Ever*, illustrated by Richard Scarry, whose picture books are all superb. Rand McNally offers *The Real Mother Goose*, illustrated with traditional pictures. The oldest Mother Goose book in the United States still in print is the Volland classic edition first published in 1915. An edition of this beautiful book, profusely illustrated by Frederick Richardson, is available through Rand McNally & Co.

Another book that might captivate him at this early "reading" stage is *Baby Farm Animals* by Garth Williams (Western Publishing). Both you and your child will have fun with the classic pop-up books with characters in the illustrations that spring up when the pages are turned. Two good books from the Random House Pop-Up Book series are the *Pop-Up Circus Book* and the *Pop-Up Sound Alikes*.

You may want to add a pop-up toy to continue the action of the book. Child Guidance makes one featuring the famous Disney characters—Mickey, Donald, Goofy, Pluto and Dumbo. To make his storybook friends pop up, your child will have to manipulate an intriguing button. He will have to twist, turn, slide, push or dial it, and by experimenting, he will find out which.

DRESSING UP DOLLS

Now that your child takes great pride in being able to begin and complete a task all by himself, he will enjoy his own "child" to care for. Dressing-up dolls are wonderful companions at this age. In addition to all the hugging and loving that young children give their soft dolls, a dressing-up doll helps the child to practice self-care chores we often take for granted. The dexterity needed to tie a shoelace, button or zipper a coat can be a slow, sometimes frustrating procedure for small hands and fingers just learning how to master fine manipulative skills. To help the child complete these dressing tasks, the doll's clothing is labeled according to the item to be fastened—the word "zipper" appears alongside a zipper; "tie" or "button" directs the child to a lace on a pocket or a button on a strap. While playing, the child can fulfill his desire to name everything in sight as he dresses his doll and will, no doubt, imitate the way his parents dress him.

• PLAYSKOOL's classic "learn to dress" dolls, *Dapper Dan* and *Dressy Bessy*, are very appealing brother and sister soft dolls. Each is wearing a colorful, sporty outfit with strings to tie, zipper to zip, buttons and snaps to fasten. All clothing is securely attached to the body of the doll so that clothing cannot be lost. The dolls are fourteen inches tall.

• CHILD GUIDANCE's happy playmate is *Sesame Street Big Bird Dress 'N Play Doll*. Big Bird is his usual friendly self anxiously waiting to be buttoned up to go out and play. He wears a green, hooded jacket with a large, safety zipper to open and close. Two patch pockets can be secured with either a button or a snap. The hood, which is sewn to the jacket, is kept snugly in place with a string tie.

• FISHER-PRICE has made a more advanced dressing-up doll. *Buttons and Toes* is a bright and cheery soft clown doll dressed in true clown finery. His clothes have five different dressing activities for the toddler to try—zipping, buttons and snaps, tying and lacing. (If lacing proves a bit too difficult now, introduce this action when hand manipulation improves.) An added surprise for the child is hidden within the clown's hat—open the zipper and out pops a bird! His toes are numbered on each foot. You can begin number recognition play by pointing first to each toe and number on the clown's foot then to the child's toe. And, since he loves to have you read nursery rhymes to him over and over again, the two of you can play "This Little Piggy Goes to Market."

BIG BIRD* DRESS 'N PLAY DOLL
Child Guidance
*Muppet Characters
©1984 Muppets, Inc.

Now that your child can walk, he is tasting the first delicious joys of independence from his parents. He no longer wants the kind of protectiveness he accepted at the age of one year. He is beginning to assert himself (and will do so even more insistently as he approaches the age of two) because he is at the threshold of so many new abilities.

What your child needs during this period is freedom to explore his environment in the only way he knows—by physical and sensory activity. The hardest thing for parents to accept is the fact that it is the normal behavior for a toddler to get into everything, to make a mess, to do things that appear destructive. Tearing pages out of a book, dropping a raw egg on the floor, banging a glass on the coffee table are not "bad" behavior—they are the toddler's way of learning about paper, eggs and glass. If you can remember that these actions are indications of his intelligence and curiosity, that he is engaged in the learning process, perhaps it will help you get through this transitional period with more equanimity.

Eighteen Months to Two Years
"I, Me, Mine"

Your child now has reached the age when he is literally "putting himself together." The ability to walk has changed the eighteen month old's perspective immensely. He has a clearer sense of self; locomotor skills enable him to satisfy his drive to explore all his surroundings; he is insatiable in his need to master language.

"I." "Me!" "Mine." Independence is the name of his game. The six-month period that begins at eighteen months has often been referred to as the "negative" period. The child's favorite word certainly is "NO." He may explode into temper tantrums when he can't have his way because he can be frustrated very easily. But, this negativism is a necessary part of your toddler's development, reflecting his increasingly strong sense of himself as a separate, independent, thinking person. This realization that he *can* choose NOT to do something heralds his emergence as his own personality.

There are positive developments during this period, too, as your child becomes more aware of people and able to enjoy new activities. And by the time he reaches his second birthday, he will have reached a point of equilibrium which will be a source of satisfaction to himself and a welcome relief to his parents.

As this period starts, the child is a run-about. Because he is quite steady on his feet, all his energy and attention are not taken up with the task of walking. Now he can do other things at the same time, such as hold a toy, carry a doll or something large and bulky, push or pull an object as he strolls about. By doing two things at one time, he is practicing the coordination of his large motor muscles and fine manual skills. His method of picking up a toy from the floor has changed. He

101

can stoop from a standing posture and pick it up instead of having to sit down, then pick the object up and stand. When he is pulling a toy behind him he can look over his shoulder as he walks. He delights in his ability to walk backward. While toddlers can start and stop walking smoothly, they are not able to turn corners with ease.

You will notice that the toddler is usually most mobile and exploratory in a familiar setting when a parent, usually the mother, is near by. As he plays, he is ever conscious of his mother's presence. She is *home base*. She gives him the courage to face the insecurity of the wider world. She is there to refer to for reassurance as he explores and to return to if the world proves alarming. Most toddlers rarely stray out of sight of their mothers.

TODDLERS' GYMS

Since gross-motor activities take precedence over fine-motor ones, toys and equipment for physical activity continue to be of primary importance. Climbing and moving large objects are favorite pursuits. He finds stair climbing irresistible. He walks up stairs; backs down on hands and knees.

TIKE TREEHOUSE
Little Tikes

• LITTLE TIKES' *Playhouse* and *Tike Treehouse* will satisfy your child's climbing, exploring and sliding instincts. Climb up three sturdy, wide steps to get to the top of the Playhouse. Then, slide down the blue ramp on the other side. Or, crawl through the tunnel under the yellow roof. It stands 30 inches high, 56 inches long and 18 inches wide and can be used indoors and out. The Treehouse provides a wide platform at the top of the stairs. The large area gives the toddler plenty of room to get ready to slide down the ramp set at a gentle angle. The Treehouse is topped by a weatherproof roof. It is built with safety in mind, offering the exploring child a place of his own from which to view his surroundings. These two toddler's gyms will prove useful and provide fun for many years to come.

BLOCKS

During the next few months, the toddler will spend time investigating the various ways of piling, building and putting things together. He is still pleased that things can be fitted together, but now he is extremely curious about how it's done. When stacking, he will experiment with the art of balancing objects. What happens when a small block is placed on top of a large one? What happens when the tower he is building is out of balance? It comes tumbling down—an event he enjoys as much as building and putting together.

You will notice, perhaps unhappily, that he has decided to re-arrange some of the furniture. He loves to push large items around. A chair is now situated by the table; a box has been moved near the sink or stove. All are waiting to be climbed.

At this stage, take another look around the house and play yard. Your toddler is very mobile and has also added several new abilities since the last time you checked the whole house for safety. Make sure that he cannot reach the controls that turn the stove on, or any electrical socket. Place sharp items, chemicals and poisonous substances out of reach, preferably hidden from the child's view.

To satisfy his urge to handle large items, offer him a set of giant blocks which are lightweight and easy to grip.

• LITTLE TIKES makes giant blocks in polyethylene with soft, rounded corners. The set comes in bold primary colors and a matte finish so that the toddler can hold and stack without the blocks slipping. The set has eight different shapes and includes ramps and a bridge.

• EICHHORN WOOD TOYS makes several sets of large stacking blocks in wood. Each set has blocks of six to eight different sizes that are decorated with ABCs, Disney characters, or storybook characters.

Some large blocks are hollow so they can be nested or stacked.

GIANT BLOCKS
Little Tikes

RIDING TOYS

Riding and rocking toys are favorites of the roaming toddler. He will hop on the Riding Horse or Tyke Bike or School Bus you have already introduced. Now he pushes his vehicle along with both feet. He won't really be able to pedal a tricycle until he is three years old. Remember, the best kiddie cars have two front wheels for extra stability. Test for balance.

Before you buy a kiddie car, turn the handle bars all the way to one side and give a forward tug. If it tips, purchase another type. Otherwise your child will be taking a lot of spills as he turns corners. Check for metal edges and loose parts. It is best to select one that is sturdy enough for outdoor play since the toddler likes to be outdoors.

Vehicles that look like the real thing will capture your child's imagination. He has experienced an outing in the family car or a ride on a plane, bus or train and will love to pretend he is doing what the grown folks do.

• LITTLE TIKES' collection of vehicles includes a *Cozy Coupe* with bright yellow roof, a driver's door that opens and closes, large tires, behind-the-seat storage compartment, easy to grip steering wheel. There is a non-removable gas cap which opens and closes to take a "fill-up" from the *Happy Pumper*. This red, smiling gas pump has a 24-inch flexible vinyl hose designed to fit into any Little Tikes' vehicle equipped with a gas cap. A crank turns to activate a bell while gallons and cents appear on the meter. Behind the pump there is a set of tune

COZY COUPE
Little Tikes

up tools (hammer and wrench) and oil and water cans to help keep the toddler's car in tiptop shape.

Another car in blue is the Little Tikes *T Car*. This does not have a roof, but has all the other features of the *Cozy Coupe*.

The *Fire Engine* by Little Tikes looks very real. There is a brass bell to ring to warn others on the road to "watch out!" A pull-out fire hose, wide seats and shiny chrome handlebars make this riding toy one your child will enjoy for several years to come.

All these riding toys are well-made with the safety of the child under two in mind. Wheels are balanced and placed so that the child can maneuver about with ease; the details stimulate any young child's imagination.

• CHILD GUIDANCE's *Ride-On Work Horse* is an advanced version of the riding horse. As an extra, there is a workbench hidden under the saddle with two pegs and two screws to pound and turn. These are large enough so that a small hand can manipulate them easily. The tools are a screwdriver and a hammer and wrench with wooden handles.

RIDE-ON WORK HORSE
Child Guidance

• FISHER-PRICE's *Hot Rod Roadster* is a sporty vehicle. The four-piece engine comes apart and can be "fixed" (put together). A push button horn makes a beep-beep sound, while large balloon tires go "clickety clack" as he races along. There is storage space under the seat for other toys. The steering column can be used to pull the racer if he tires of riding.

• TOMY's *Stubby Space Shuttle* is the latest in a riding vehicle. Control decals on the steering wheel and rocket cluster in back will make him feel as if he is just taking off for a trip to outer space . . . as long as you are going along, of course.

The toddler still loves his pull toys which take on added interest with his new ability to walk backwards and sideways. As he does, he wants to hold onto something—the pull toy, a stuffed animal or doll, a small block.

The toddler approaching two is apt to spend more of his time playing with toys than he did during the previous months. He will contently play alone for longer periods of time (20 to 30 minutes), if he knows that his mother or father is close by.

He is becoming more and more aware of textures. The feel of water and sand will absolutely captivate him. Combine these two elements with filling and dumping activities and you have the toddler's idea of perfect bliss.

HOT ROD ROADSTER
Fisher-Price Toys

WATER and SAND TOYS

Sand shovels, sifters, funnels, pouring containers of various sizes will allow him to experiment with the flowing qualities of sand and water. Add water to the sand and he will be able to discover the packing qualities of the wet and dry combination.

HP TOYS and BERCHET have a collection of colorful water and sand toys. *Sand Set* includes a large shovel with sand molds to make animal, boat and other figures in the sand. Berchet's *Tree-Shaped Sieve* set holds a rack, shovel and five sand molds. Their *Fit-Together Boat* is unique in that it converts from a boat into a sand bucket. When he is finished playing with one, he can play with the other.

The child who has had experience with sand and mud will be ready, as he nears the age of two, for related art materials such as *Play-Doh* and finger paints.

CRAYONS

The toddler will also like to play with crayons.

The 18-month-old child not only makes a mark on the paper placed before him but also scribbles. Before this age, when offered a crayon he would probably "hit" the crayon against the paper, making dots. There was no real understanding of the relationship between the crayon and the paper.

Give him a jumbo crayon—there are several makes on the market, but Crayola is the established brand. Your child will enjoy his first set of eight jumbos introduced at this age, and he will eventually grow up to the box of 64 containing a rainbow of hues. Provide fairly large sheets of paper—you can create your own free supply of paper by cutting up and using large supermarket bags or old newspapers.

The child's main interests will be scribbling and making marks at random. Researchers studying adaptive behavior report that the directions of the marks or scribbles made by toddlers of this age group are varied. Some make horizontal lines, while others will opt for vertical lines. Many of his markings will go off the page. He will develop the ability to draw a circle later.

Researchers have also found that drawing is not a spontaneous act for the toddler. He does not just pick up the crayon or pencil and begin to draw. He needs to be shown that if he maneuvers his crayon in a certain way he can make a line. When he discovers that he is the instigator of the colorful marks on the paper, he will take great pride in making more and more. The ability to hold a crayon and write or draw is peculiar to humans. It is this particular action (the pincer grip) that separates us from the other animals. When your child scribbles, he is creating a mark unique to himself. It is an idea . . . the beginning of an idea. By praising him for his efforts and hanging his "painting," you will be encouraging him to try again. Free experimentation will be his style. He will get into figures and more intricate line drawings during the preschool years.

Talk to him about the colors of the crayons as he pulls them out of the box. You can match these basic colors to the colors of his toys which are also painted in the primary hues. His first box of crayons will probably include red, orange, yellow, green, blue, violet, white and black.

Your child is developing a sense of logic as he enters the age of problem-solving. During this six-month period, the child makes great advances in his intellectual capacity as his memory span increases and verbal competence grows. At the same time, he is becoming more adept in the use of his hands. This advance in both mental and manipulative abilities means that a number of early-learning toys can be introduced now.

SHAPE SORTERS

Foremost among the more advanced toys is a shape-sorting box, one of the absolute essentials for every child. The lid of the box has holes of four or five different shapes, each designed to accommodate a correspondingly shaped block. This is an early version of one in a series of toys for shape discrimination. It will satisfy the toddler's continuing interest in filling and dumping, in handling little objects one at a time, and in making things disappear and reappear. It helps him learn the relationship between shapes (the blocks) and negative shapes (the holes). The skills he learns are among those necessary for the visual shape discrimination required in reading.

In selecting a shape-sorting device, be sure to choose one that your child can open by himself.

Avoid toys that have shapes that are too difficult to differentiate— such as a six-pointed star or a seven-pointed star. The most important shapes for beginners are the circle, square and triangle. The next shapes to be added might include a rectangle, a semicircle, an oval or one odd-shaped piece. Make sure, too, that a block cannot be manuevered or forced into the wrong hole. In order for the shape sorter to be a learning device, it must be self-correcting. This means that each block must fit *only* into its corresponding hole and only when it is held in the proper position.

A shape-sorting box teaches the toddler on several levels. When he is trying to place the square or triangle in the square or triangular hole, he is exercising his judgment. He is working with perspective and dimension. Learning to differentiate among various shapes, colors and sizes will help him during his early school years to tell the difference between letters and numbers. As we mentioned, children love to solve problems. This type of toy will build his power of concentration. Watch as he attempts to fit the square shape into the round hole . . . "No, that's not the one," he decides. "Let's try this hole." Success! "It fits!"

Because he is a great imitator of adult actions, you may want to help him get started by playing with him. Show him a shape, the triangle for instance. Name it for him. You can put it directly into the right hole or you can make a mistake. Either way, illustrate through your actions how the two right shapes relate to one another. He is not apt to obey verbal commands since he does not understand the full meaning of them as yet, but he will grasp what you are showing him.

However, be careful not to introduce a problem-solving toy beyond the child's capabilities. It will frustrate him and, probably, turn him off completely. If he gets tired or wants to stop, put the toy away for awhile and bring it out later.

• BRIO has the classic shape-sorting box. The natural wooden box is fitted with a red lid that has squares, triangular and circular openings. Six blocks in three shapes and colors will provide the challenge.

• AMBI's *Shape Box* features eight fundamental shapes with matching holes. In addition to the usual square, triangle and circle, there is a star, a cross, a rectangle, a half circle and a six-sided piece. The lid is removable for the continuous process of filling and dumping.

• FISCHERFORM has designed a shape sorter that consists of 12 brightly colored rattle blocks in different shapes. This container, unlike the others, is clear so that your child can see the blocks pile up as he drops each piece through the correct slot.

Shape sorters also come in untraditional forms.

• KIDDICRAFT's *Hippo Shape Sorter* holds six assorted pieces. His mouth opens to remove the shapes. Hippo doubles as a pull-along toy, and that marvelous mouth opens and shuts as he is pulled along.

• PLAYSKOOL's *Teddy Bear Shape Sorter* has six different shapes that fit into matching openings around the bear's middle. Lift his jaunty yellow hat to retrieve the blocks.

• CHILD GUIDANCE's *Shapey Turtle* offers the toddler seven shapes to fit. Once they find their way into the shell of the turtle, lift it up and start over again.

• PLAYSKOOL's traditional sorter is the *Postal Station*. The red, white and blue mailbox is a bit more advanced in that the child must turn a key to open the mailbox door to retrieve the shapes. But, this familiar object is fun because the child can imagine that he is mailing letters of various shapes to his best friends.

TEDDY BEAR SHAPE SORTER
Playskool

Brio has manufactured two variations of the shape sorter called threaders. The pieces to be matched to the holes are attached to the main unit with strings. (There is the advantage that there are no loose pieces that can be lost.) In the first version, there is a string of beads or small cubes that can be pushed through the center hole of a red disc. In a more complex version, the disc has three hole with different shapes—a circle, a square and a triangle. The string of spheres, cubes and triangles is matched to the correct hole and pushed through. With these toys, the concept learned is "through" rather than "into" as with the shape-sorting boxes. This is practice for the special coordination required in bead-stringing, an important activity beginning at about the age of two.

Another kind of learning toy for the eighteen-month-old is the *Peg Leveler* (Whitney Bros. Co., Malborough, N.H. 03455). It consists of a base, with four holes of graduated depth and four pegs of graduated length. The object is to insert the pegs into the holes in such a way that the tops are all level. It take considerable trial and error to find the right combination because the depth cannot be judged without actual testing. Perhaps your child will discover that he can test the depths of the holes and pegs with his finger rather than making random trials. The manufacturer has wisely kept all the pegs a natural wood color so that the comparisons must be made by length alone—there's no color-coding to cue the child.

TAKE APART TOYS

Slightly more complex stacking toys than those used at one year may be introduced now—the toddler still likes toys that have to be taken apart and put together.

There are advanced versions of the color cone which may have as many as fifteen discs on the spindle. Some stacking toys may have discs with unusual shapes and angles or the pieces may stack together to form a clown or an animal figure.

• BRIO's collection of take-apart, stackable figures are beautifully made. Each amusing figure (*Freddy, Clown, Puck The Dog, Max Dachshund, Ring Pyramid*) has a number of parts in vivid colors—red, green, blue, yellow and black. The bodies are made of a set of graduating rings.

Simple take-apart and put-together toys satisfy the urge the child has to handle, investigate and manipulate things. These toys teach him shape, sizing, dimension and depth as well as how to reach, grasp and pull apart.

He is learning how things work. He is solving a problem. After he has taken the toy apart, he must figure how to put it together again into the original shape. He is learning the important intellectual concept of reversability—that which can be taken apart, can also be reconstructed.

These toys can be used for story-telling. On command, point to and name the parts of his body. As you play with him, ask him to point to his nose, eyes, head, leg, mouth and so forth. Then, as he is playing with his take apart toy, go into the same routine:

"Where is the clown's head (hat)?"

"Where are the doggy's ears? Look how long they are."

"Show me where this piece goes on the Pyramid. Look at this pretty blue ring."

As you go, add a phrase about dimension, size or color. Language is now becoming a means of communicating ideas and information, not just a way to satisfy immediate needs.

It is interesting to note that researchers vary on theories about how children learn to speak—whether the comprehension of a word must come before that word can be spoken, or whether the word can be spoken before it is understood. Child development experts do agree on one point: the importance of language.

"It is the most vital function which an infant develops," says Penelope Leach in her book, *Babyhood*. "It is the basic tool of being a human being, . . . even though language learning can continue throughout childhood, it is clear that the first two years comprise the optimum time for its foundation to be laid."

Ms. Leach adds, "The infant's eventual production of words comes about more by watching the mother, and listening to her constant use of the word-related-to-the-object, than by her direct teaching."

O.H. Mowrer writes in his article "Hearing and Speaking: An Analysis of Language Learning," *Journal of Speech and Hearing Disorders,* 1969, that a child hearing his own sounds is stimulated to make further sounds. The more affectionate the context in which his first sounds (from the outside world) are heard, the more he will make them himself, and be stimulated to make more. Early babbling and later, "jargoning" almost always occur when a child is pleased. It also seems from collective findings during testing, that the child's (infant's) eventual production of words comes about "more by watching the mother (parent) and listening to her constant use of the word-related-to-the-object, than by her direct teaching." Therefore the child may learn far more from observation and word interplay than he does by having an object (book, shoe, toy) dangled in front of him while the mother says "Book. Say, Book."

• AMBI makes *Ringle Bell*, another pyramid shape take-apart toy. A bell is the added feature in this pyramid with its six circular rings in graduated size and variety of colors. The knob on the top screws onto a central post to keep everything in place.

• KOUVALIAS also has a wide range of figure stacking toys. One resembles a modern figure—an astronaut.

NEST AND STACK TOYS

Sorting and arranging continue to hold the toddler's interest. The combination is found in nesting and stacking toys which make good first building sets. You have already introduced several such sets—most with just a few pieces. Now that your child is able to stack about six cubes, you can introduce him to some more complex nest and stack sets.

The toddler's wrist action is improving. Now he can turn or screw a lid onto a cup shaped object, which he is able to hold with considerable skill. He is able to manipulate objects with both hands. He can pass objects from one hand to another more easily and he is able to drink from a cup, holding it, at times, with one hand.

• AMBI offers the most versatile selection of nest and stack toys:

Handy Boxes comes in six sizes in six primary colors, each with its own lid to take off and put on.

Drums, eight pot-like containers—sized from tiny to large—stack snugly on top of one another.

Color Cups provide ten numbered beakers—each in a different size and color—that nest and stack.

Nesting Beakers are twelve nesting and building cups in a variety of colors with recessed outer rims for easy stacking.

Top Cubes and *Nesting Cubes* give your toddler ten square cups with rounded corners that have recessed tops for stacking and eight cubes with the same features. Each size has a different color and is numbered.

All of the above sets are easy to handle. Your toddler can build tall, sturdy towers that won't fall over until he decides he would like to see all come tumbling down. The vivid color produces a very satisfactory looking tower. Reverse the procedure and your child will wind up with a neatly nested set of cubes or boxes. This toy will absorb him entirely as he puts all his efforts and concentration into fitting the objects together.

Don't be too surprised if he scatters the pieces over the floor before and after he finishes playing. Part of the fun is the continuous action of towers going up, objects disappearing into each other and, finally, everything being scattered all over the place. Because of the graduated sizes he will become aware of balance and size order. These toys provide the same play action as his block set—proper placement is crucial for stacking success.

• LEGO *Building Brick Sets* have stirred the imagination of older children for years. If you have not introduced the DUPLO *Block Sets* to your toddler, now is the time to do so. DUPLO parts are similar and interchangeable with LEGO sets, but geared to the abilities of the toddler. Each set contains large-sized blocks with smooth, rounded corners. Each set is made of the LEGO set colors and includes people and pet figures that snap into place.

DUPLO sets in the *Rattle 'n Roll* series contain wheeled platforms so that the child can push or pull the toy he has created. In the starter sets mentioned in the previous chapter, the wheeled platform comes with a built-in rattle. One platform also rocks back and forth with a see-saw effect.

The fantasy DUPLO *Playville* sets present a theme to challenge the child's imagination and creativity. These more complex sets contain 21 to 66 pieces. *Playville Barnyard* (21 pieces) features farm animals (horse, sheep, rooster) plus a farmer, windmill and haywagon. The child can build a fence for his animals with pieces that are available. He can add the Pony Trailer to this scene. *Playville Nursery School* (29 pieces) includes a teacher, pupils, blackboard, clock with hands that move, school bus and bell that rings to bring the kids to school. There are DUPLO *Basic Building* Sets which include extra pieces—door and window blocks, oval, arch and beam blocks—to expand existing sets.

**BUILDING BLOCK SYSTEM
DUPLO**

The play value offered in the DUPLO and LEGO sets is unlimited. The toy becomes whatever the child creates, changing each time he picks up his blocks and builds again. His assurance grows as he is able to carry tasks to completion. You will notice that when a toddler experiences the satisfaction of something working, he will smile, clap his hands, laugh and feel good all over. It is only when he is frustrated that he cries and shrieks.

PUZZLES

First puzzles with a few pieces either in wood or woodboard offer shape-and-pattern discrimination practice. He will like to solve the problem presented—to match shape to shape, color to color, object to object. This sort of quiet time activity helps develop fitting, discriminating and recognition skills.

• PLAYSKOOL makes a series of first puzzles with 4 to 7 pieces. Subjects familiar to the toddler are illustrated on each large piece. He can match the piece and the space to create Colors, Pets, Things That Fly, Farm Animals, My House, Picnic and so on.

Puzzles with large wooden pieces fitted with hardwood knobs are also excellent first puzzles. The knob makes it easy to grasp the puzzle piece. Some have pieces that are free-standing and can be used as toys in themselves.

DELUXE WOOD PUZZLES
Fisher-Price Toys

• The TOYS TO GROW ON catalog features *Big Knob Shape Board* with large 2⅛ inch mushroom-shaped knobs fitted onto six different pieces. These shapes, in turn, fit into matching cut-out spaces on the puzzle base.

• FISHER-PRICE's *Pick Up & Peek* wooden puzzles also feature easy-to-lift knobs. These puzzles help the child to practice a number of problem-solving skills. Each illustrated piece covers a surprise picture for the child to find when he lifts the piece. To test his abilities he can try to make two matches—puzzle shape to the opening on the board; and the puzzle picture to a scene on the board. In addition, since the puzzle pieces stand alone, they can be used individually during imaginative play.

• ACRE puzzles, similar in design, also have wooden pieces fitted with knobs. Their *Inset Boards* are best at this age. Each puzzle shows the same object (house, tree, flower, cat, car, apple) in various sizes and slightly different shapes. You will want to help him with these since the puzzle is more sophisticated and more advanced than the usual first puzzle. But your child has made great strides in noticing small details and will enjoy pointing the differences out to you as you help him.

Take advantage of the fact that as he approaches two years of age, his manipulative skills, eye-hand coordination and ability to name things are improving at a rapid pace. His attention span is still short. He may play with the puzzle, pick up and fit several pieces, and then walk away to come back to it in a little while. He loves repetition and the challenge of completion that the puzzle offers him.

He is able to identify objects and place them accurately, i.e., shoe on his foot. He is beginning to think symbolically, storing and remembering images and ideas. For example, if he left his toy in the living room behind a chair and then went outdoors to play, upon his return he will be able to retrieve the toy because he remembered where he put it. He is beginning to realize that items may be related and possess common qualities; balls are round and bounce, but individually they may be different in size, color and weight.

As he plays with a variety of toys and other objects, he is building his storehouse of information from which he will increasingly draw as his intellect and creativity grow and develop.

Puzzle and problem-solving toys give the child a chance to practice eye-hand coordination—he recognizes the correct puzzle piece and puts it in its proper place. He learns spatial relationships, develops powers of concentration and exercises the small muscles of his fingers. And by concentrating on the puzzles for longer and longer periods of time, he is increasing his attention span. In addition, as he scans the puzzle for the proper opening, his eyes constantly moving back and forth, he is practicing reading skills. The same motion is used in reading. Watching TV, for instance, does not involve the scanning motion necessary for successful reading skills.

Puzzles also help develop problem-solving skills. Each time he places a piece that fits he has solved a problem. The child receives a tremendous feeling of accomplishment when he has been able to complete a puzzle.

Language, creativity, imagination, imitation all lend themselves to dramatic play. Now the toddler is talking to his toy in his own language. He is imitating your talking on the telephone or cooking or sweeping the floor or wearing adult clothes like shoes, etc. He is a little actor acting out all sorts of roles, and he is creating his own material.

MAKE-BELIEVE TOYS

Your child will now be able to tackle toys that present multiple play opportunities. These toys take into consideration the combined abilities the toddler possesses now. Imaginatively, he can participate in the scene of the toy, such as a village, a farm, a schoolyard.

• JOHNSON & JOHNSON's *Peg Pals Village* is a perfect example. This set has all kinds of fascinating possibilities for fun and fantasy play. Peg Pals combine with other pieces to make a tall tower. Peg Pals fit into cars and drive around the village. Blocks and triangular pieces can be put together to form houses. The entire scene can be arranged and rearranged to create a new environment every day.

JOHNSON & JOHNSON offers *Storybook Playsets*, another fantasy playset. This set comes with a soft book about a Firehouse, School or Zoo which turns into a three-dimensional setting. The book buildings represent the main theme of the story. Peg characters and a vehicle are included in the playset. Each theme helps the child learn an important concept: Firehouse—Don't play with matches and Help others. *Peg Pals Go To School* helps the child prepare for the nursery school or day care center experience; *Peg Pals Visit The Zoo* helps the child become familiar with animals and the zoo setting.

Keep the DUPLO *Playville Farm* and *Nursery School Sets* handy for such creative play.

The toddler is learning to use toys as objects in fantasy play, in creating scenarios that involve ideas. He is seeking toys that offer a wider variety of experiences instead of just one like stacking, fitting or pulling along. He now controls his environment and can anticipate what his toy may do if he touches it in a certain way. Instead of wondering if the pieces in the sorting box will fall out when the container is tipped upside down, he will begin to anticipate what the

PEG PALS VILLAGE
Johnson & Johnson

STORYBOOK PLAYSETS
Johnson & Johnson

consequences of his actions will be. He will transform his toys into a make-believe environment that he can control.

Somewhere around twenty-one months, toddlers become familiar with the concept of personal possession. Words mean more to them as they are connected with objects in their own home. They are able to name almost all the items that they see and handle on a daily basis. Therefore, they very vociferously claim ownership of the things that belong to them—toys, mainly. You will hear "ME" and "MINE" quite a lot through the day. And, what a wonderful sound! You child is very much aware of himself. His self-importance, hence self-esteem, is passionately proclaimed.

Child development experts place a great deal of emphasis on building self-esteem. Once the child is confident about his actions and abilities—that HE CAN make something happen, then he is wide open to all kinds of learning experiences. He does not have to spend so much time and energy impressing others. Instead he can spend his days hungrily taking in the wonders of the world about him.

The concept of personal possession also marks the beginning of a period when the child forms a deep attachment to a special toy, a cuddly doll or even a blanket. Shades of Linus! He may be unable to sleep or travel or go anywhere without it tucked under his arm. Accidentally leaving it behind is a disaster.

You will notice that the child of this age begins to play NEAR other children, but still doesn't play WITH them. This is termed "parallel play." He is also totally selfish with his playthings and not about to share anything with anyone. So don't despair. He does not have bad character; you have not missed the boat somewhere during these past two years.He is merely establishing "self" and possession.

During the next few months, however, he becomes increasingly aware of other people around him, both children and adults. He will especially enjoy imitating the everyday activities of his parents and he will imitate the play activities of older children. He will like to sweep and dust and enjoy using your broom or dustpan and brush. A toy telephone is a must at this age because it will encourage his using and learning language.

There are several toddler telephones with faces as part of the dial and parts that squeak or make a ringing sound. Ambi makes one with several interesting features. The handset has a funny face on one end and an unbreakable mirror on the other. He will enjoy jabbering away to his friend.

STEERING WHEEL TOYS

Driving intrigues him. Steering-wheel toys and vehicles, especially those which offer several play activities in addition to being pushed or pulled along, will satisfy his urge to imitate you.

Steering-wheel toys also come in different designs and degrees of complexity. Basically, the child sits behind the car dashboard which comes complete with a steering wheel, horn, ignition key and rear view mirror.

• CHILD GUIDANCE combines the driving toy with the magic of electronic sounds. Their *Supersound Driver* is battery operated. A key starts the motor, then he pushes the gear shift to "rev" up the engine. The steering wheel turns and "beeps." A lever flashes the directional signals. A rear view safety mirror and pretend radio with station selector dial complete the realistic auto. The driving console fits right over the child's lap so that he feels that he is really driving through the living room or play yard at a high rate of speed. When he is driving in the car with Dada, he can really zoom along.

SUPERSOUND DRIVER
Child Guidance

• LITTLE TIKES' *Play Transporter* turns into a very fascinating driving play set. It is actually three toys in one—a trailer truck, a bridge and a driving set. The trailer opens up to form a bridge and tunnel. The tunnel, in turn, acts as a two car garage. When the Transporter is hinged together to form the truck, the tunnel opening holds the car. A most imaginative play truck.

• JOHNSON & JOHNSON's *Stack & Dump Truck* is also designed to create a number of learning opportunities. Yellow and blue chips can be stacked on pegs in the cargo bay or deposited into piggy-bank-like slots where they disappear. The round chips fit over the headlights; the square ones fit over the hubcaps. Under the cargo area is a storage place for chips between playtimes. Two smiling bears are driving the truck.

STACK AND DUMP TRUCK
Johnson & Johnson

As the toddler advances in identifying numbers, the *Chicco School Bus* becomes a very useful and versatile toy. He will begin by pushing the bus along with its array of children's faces peering out the window. Twelve bags of luggage stack neatly on top of the bus. Later, as he is learning how to count, he can load the passenger onto the bus one by one by pressing a button. The faces move along the windows as he pushes the button, and, finally, a number appears in the front of the bus to show how many passengers have boarded.

• CHILD GUIDANCE *Push 'N Pull Tractor and Trailer Playset* is an example of a toy with a combination of play opportunities: it is a sorting and nesting toy, a push and pull-along vehicle and a fantasy plaything. Twelve pieces make up the farm theme of the playset which includes a farmer and his wife, four barnyard animals and four fence pieces to assemble. The animals fit neatly into notches on the trailer. The farmer and his wife sit in front in the tractor.

RECORDS

The nearly-two-year-old is sensitive to music and has tremendous appreciation for it. He responds to rhythm with his whole body. You will find him dancing and swaying about to the sounds of the radio or the phonograph, and he will follow and imitate the action of a dancer on TV.

A record player would be a good investment at this time. You may have to play it for him at first, but many children can operate a record player by themselves before the age of two. There was a time when children's record players were simple, one-speed (78 rpm) affairs. But these days so many children's records are LPs that you will want to buy a three-speed player. You can expect it to serve for many years.

Record-playing is a nice transition from playtime to naptime, and there are some children and parents who like records in addition to the traditional bedtime story at night. There is no substitute for holding a child cozily in your arms and telling him a story at bedtime, but records can be delightful and comforting.

Record catalogs and lists may be obtained by writing to A.A. Records, Inc. (manufacturer of Golden Records), 250 West 57 Street, New York, New York 10019, or the Children's Record Guild and Young People's Records, Inc., both at 225 Park Avenue South, New York, New York 10003. You might also look for *Recordings for Children: A Selected List*, now out of print but available in many libraries.

Several specific albums we can suggest are Frank Luther's two collections of nursery rhymes and his *Mother Goose*, all on the Decca label; *Songs to Grow On for Mother and Child* (Folkways); and the *Golden Treasury of Mother Goose and Nursery Songs* (Golden LP).

Your child will be delighted if you sing to him and with him—whether or not you feel you have a voice. And there are many beginners' song books you will enjoy together. Among the ones you might consider are the *Golden Song Book* by Katherine T. Wessells and the *New Golden Song Book* by Norman Lloyd (both by Western Publishing), *Songs to Sing to the Very Young* by P. B. Ohanian (Random House) and the old favorite *Singing Time* by S. N. Coleman and A. Thorn (John Day). Any of these books could provide many hours of family fun.

American Folk Songs For Children sung by Pete Seeger are favorite work and play songs that will encourage the young child to clap and sing along. *Walk Like The Animals* is a collection of music that imitates the way animals walk—puppy, bear, duck, crab, seal and many others.

If your child seems to be particularly interested in music, think of giving him his own simple musical instrument. Look for a sturdy version in miniature of the xylophone, a simple horn, reed flute, piano or a drum that is light enough to be carried on a strap around your child's neck for marching. Musically endowed or not, your child will love bells, whistles and resonant things on which to toot and to bang out simple rhythms.

BOOKS

For his rapidly developing language skills, you will want to add a greater variety of books to his little library. New books are published almost daily, so check your local library, bookstores and toy stores to see what the latest offerings are for the young child. You might also consult the folder *Aids to Choosing Books for Your Children*, revised annually by the Children's Book Council, Inc., 175 Fifth Avenue, New York, New York 10010. Nancy Larrick's *A Parent's Guide to Children's Reading* is a comprehensive guide for children up to twelve years.

Two helpful guides to choosing books for young children are: *Booklist* by the American Library Association, children's section and *Choosing Books For Children: A Commonsense Guide* by Betsy Hearne. Or, refer to an excellent book catalog published by Eeyore's Books for Children, 2252 Broadway, New York, N.Y. 10024. Their listing is up to date and includes a selection of records and cassettes too.

A good librarian can also be of enormous help in suggesting books that are right for your child's age and interests.

Take the opportunity to visit a good neighborhood book store that specializes in children's books. Your child will take great pride in choosing a book of his own. Show him only a few at a time so as not to cause too much confusion. He will excitedly point and gesture at the one that catches his eye . . . "Me want," he might exclaim!

At this age, the thing that still fascinates your child most about books is the discovery of familiar objects. He loves listening to a favorite story over and over again. In fact, if you read the story differently the fourth time around, he will let you know. Your child probably likes being asked to find things in the book's illustrations. He spots a known object, studies it carefully, points to the picture, looks up at you and touches your finger to the picture as he announces his find. He points again and demands, "What?" to get you to name the object he does not recognize. His vocabulary is increasing from some twenty words at 18 months to well over 50 at two years of age . . . and is growing rapidly. He understands more than 100 words. He speaks in two or three word phrases.

He does not imitate your language, but is "logically" putting his own together. "Want cookie," "All gone," "bye bye," "go there." He is building thought symbols (a hammer bangs, bird sings) and creating new ideas. According to linguists, "Growth of meaning is a highly complex interaction of learning and social factors."

Some specialists who use the environmentalist approach to language acquisition believe that the speech in the child's environment serves as the model upon which the child bases his own speech. Modeling has been found to be the most effective means of helping a child expand his use of language. Therefore talk, sing and read to your child as often as you can.

Some teaching books to use about all the things your child has learned to identify during the past two years are *Baby's Things, Words To Say, My First Book of Colors, Baby's First Toys,* Richard Scarry's *Early Words* series, Brimax's *Look & Find* series.

Short rhymes with interesting sounds, such as "Polly Put the Kettle On," will also intrigue him. You can either recall the ones you knew as a child or select from the many books of nursery rhymes.

He will also still love the activity books. Western Publishing offers the *Touch Me Book* to help him become aware of the feel of different surfaces—rough-smooth, hard-soft and the *Look, Look Book* in which he can work a see-saw, turn a wheel and operate other interesting devices. The same company publishes the *Who Lives Here?* book, with animals hidden in their homes. Indeed, any books dealing with animals delight children. There are hundreds to select from. Among the animal books worth your consideration are two books by Art Seiden: *Kittens* and *Puppies* (Grosset & Dunlap) and the *Animal Picture Book* (Platt & Munk).

So here you are, preparing for that second birthday party. It hardly seems possible, does it? Just a short twenty-four months ago you brought home that tiny, helpless bundle from the hospital, and now, suddenly, here he is running everywhere, getting into everything, never missing a trick, talking nonstop. And, he's well on the way toward taking care of his own needs: feeding, dressing, regulating and amusing himself.

As he enters his third year, he will have achieved equilibrium in several areas. Physically, he doesn't fall often; linguistically, he can make his needs known verbally—which means that he cries less; and, emotionally, he can tolerate brief frustrations and waiting periods. He still has much to learn and far go to during the remaining preschool years. His playthings and activities take on even more importance as his number of options increases.

As you played with him during the past two years, you have been instrumental in helping him reinforce the many skills and the knowledge he has acquired. You have seen him reach out to try a new experience, then retreat to seek out your help and comfort when something did not go quite right. The toys you provided were "props" for the activities that stimulated his learning processes. The parent is the child's first and most important teacher, helping him discover who he is, what he can do, how he can achieve his goals. And, you have done all of this with a great deal of love and patience. It is a very exciting partnership!

Perhaps you feel a little sad along with your exhilaration at his incredible progress. Maybe you think as he ventures out on his own he will need you less and less. You are not alone. Every mother and father who have ever lived have faced the conflict between wanting to keep their baby dependent on them and wanting him to grow up and be an independent, self-reliant person.

You'll feel the same mixture of emotions on his first day of school, when he graduates, even on his wedding day. But every parent also learns to begin to let go of the child when it is time. He will still need you for many years to come—to guide him and to love him. And, he will *always* need your confidence in him.

From the mobile dangling over his head which introduced him to bright, cheery colors and fluttery movements. . . .

From the crib gym and rattle which gave baby something to reach out to grasp tightly. . . .

From the cause and effect toy which stimulated his instinct to explore more and more. . . .

From the box with the interesting shapes and long dowel which helped him practice organization by "putting into" and "fitting onto". . . .

From the funny looking creature that could be pulled and pushed along the floor. . . .

From the wooden horse or noisy toy truck that he propelled under his own steam. . . .

From the delightful discovery of the pretty picture in a book. . . .

From the soft doll he hugs and loves dearly. . . .

To a very special, unique, distinctive two year old who has put a myriad of individual skills together so that he can do everything . . . "*all by myself.*"

THE END

Month By Month Play Chart

Each month you will discover that your baby's development will change rapidly, sometimes radically, overnight. One day he CAN'T put one block atop another, speak or walk. The very next day he CAN! The following Play Chart outlines the baby's development month by month and suggests playthings that will be satisfying and challenging.

BIRTH TO 1 MONTH
Babies like to:
 SUCK
 LISTEN to repeated soft sounds
 STARE at movement and light
 Be HELD and ROCKED

Give your baby:
 Your TALKING and SINGING
 LAMPS throwing light patterns
 Your ARMS

1 MONTH
Babies like to:
 LISTEN to your voice
 LOOK up and to the side
 HOLD things placed in their hands

Give your baby:
 A lullaby RECORD
 A MOBILE overhead
 PICTURES on the walls
 Your FACE near his

2 MONTHS
Babies like to:
 LISTEN to musical sounds
 FOCUS, especially on their hands
 REACH and BAT nearby objects
 SMILE

Give your baby:
 A MUSIC BOX or a soft MUSICAL TOY
 A soft security CUDDLE TOY tied to crib
 Your SMILE

3 MONTHS
Babies like to:
 REACH and FEEL with open hands
 GRASP crudely with two hands
 WAVE their fists and WATCH them

Give your baby:
 MUSICAL RECORDS
 RATTLES
 DANGLING TOYS

4 MONTHS
Babies like to:
 GRASP things and LET GO
 KICK
 LAUGH at unexpected sights and sounds
 Make CONSONANT SOUNDS

Give your baby:
 BELLS tied to their crib
 A CRIB GYM
 More DANGLING TOYS

5 MONTHS
Babies like to:
 SHAKE, FEEL and BANG things
 SIT with support
 PLAY PEEK-A-BOO
 ROLL over

Give your baby:
 A HIGH CHAIR with a rubber SUCTION TOY
 A PLAY PEN
 A KICKING TOY

6 MONTHS
Babies like to:
SHAKE, BANG and THROW THINGS DOWN
GUM objects
RECOGNIZE familiar FACES

Give your baby:
Many HOUSEHOLD OBJECTS
Tin CUPS, SPOONS and pot LIDS
Wire WHISKS
A CLUTCH BALL and SQUEAKY TOYS
A TEETHER and GUMMING TOYS

7 MONTHS
Babies like to:
SIT alone
USE their FINGERS and THUMB
NOTICE CAUSE and EFFECT
BITE on their FIRST TOOTH

Give your baby:
BATH TUB TOYS
More 'THINGS'
STRING
More SQUEAKY TOYS

8

B

MADISON COUNTY-
CANTON PUBLIC
LIBRARY

PRESENTS

Concerts
1992-93

October 18
Keith Pettway
flute

November 22
Joel Harrison

EMSELVES UP

ings generally where they're wanted
DA''
-A-CAKE

y:
CORNER of the room to EXPLORE
TOYS tied to his HIGH CHAIR
A metal MIRROR
A JACK-IN-THE-BOX

10 MONTHS
Babies like to:
POKE and PROD with their forefingers
PUT THINGS IN other things
IMITATE SOUNDS

Give your baby:
A big PEG BOARD
Some CLOTH BOOKS
MOTION TOYS

11 MONTHS TO 1 YEAR
Babies like to:
USE their FINGERS
LOWER THEMSELVES from standing
DRINK from a cup
MARK on a paper

Give your baby:
PYRAMID DISCS
A large CRAYON
A baking TIN with CLOTHES PINS
His own DRINKING CUP

1 YEAR TO 13 MONTHS
Babies like to:
CREEP
CRUISE
USE 1 or 2 WORDS
USE their FINGERS
Be HUGGED

Give your baby:
A BABYPROOF HOUSE
CUDDLING
A STACKING TOWER

13 MONTHS
Babies like to:
STAND UP, SIT DOWN
Try FEEDING themselves
RELEASE OBJECTS with more precision
IMITATE YOU
Play WHERE'S BABY

Give your baby:
His own DISH, CUP, SPOON
Your GAMES with him
FITTING TOYS

14 MONTHS
Babies like to:
Put SOUNDS together
Have an AUDIENCE
SEARCH for hidden toys
PILE 2 or 3 blocks

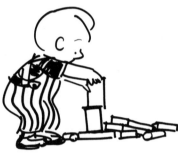

Give your baby:
Your ATTENTION
WOOD BLOCKS
A CONTAINER TOY

15 MONTHS
Babies like to:
WALK ALONE
FLING objects
FILL and EMPTY
RESPOND to KEY WORDS
Exercise HAND SKILLS

Give your baby:
Big OUTDOOR TOYS
Your CONVERSATION
MANIPULATIVE TOYS

16 MONTHS
Babies like to:
SQUAT DOWN
Walk CARRYING things
Use SAND
ROUGH-HOUSE

Give your baby:
PUSH and PULL TOYS
Big SOFT TOYS
Indoor or outdoor SANDBOX
YOU on the FLOOR

17 MONTHS
Babies like to:
LUG, TUG, DRAG things
WAVE BYE-BYE
Use WATER
Get INTO EVERYTHING

Give your baby:
WATER and POURING TOYS
HAMMERING TOYS
Your WATCHFULNESS
Bigger PULL TOYS

18 MONTHS

Babies like to:
  OPPOSE YOU with "NO"
  GET what they want NOW
  Use WORDS with GESTURES
  CLIMB STAIRS

Give your baby:
  Your DIPLOMACY
  STAIRS
  A toy TELEPHONE
  Cloth PICTURE BOOKS

19 MONTHS

Babies like to:
  CLIMB UP onto everything
  MOVE to MUSIC
  IDENTIFY parts of themselves
  SORT OBJECTS and SHAPES

Give your baby:
  A SHAPE SORTING BOX
  A RECORD PLAYER out of reach

20 MONTHS

Babies like to:
  FETCH and CARRY
  DIG and MESS
  Have things THEIR WAY
  REMEMBER from yesterday
  TAKE things APART
  USE 15 to 20 WORDS

Give your baby:
  A carrying CASE
  Little CHORES
  Your PATIENCE
  THINGS to take apart

21 MONTHS

Babies like to:
  Claim "MINE"
  MARK on PAPER
  POINT to objects in BOOK
  TURN PAGES
  FIT things TOGETHER

Give your baby:
  A big CRAYON and PAPER
  PICTURE BOOKS
  A CONSTRUCTION SET

22 MONTHS

Babies like to:
  FIT SHAPES
  WATCH GROWNUPS
  PUT things BACK
  COME when CALLED
  SCREW and UNSCREW

Give your baby:
  SHELVES for his toys
  HELP in putting things away
  Simple PUZZLES
  A plastic JAR with screw LID

23 MONTHS TO 2 YEARS

Babies like to:
  Use 3 WORD SENTENCES
  RUN
  HELP with household tasks
  Hear RHYMES
  Work with their FINGERS

Give your baby:
  A DOLL or TEDDY
  A TOY to RIDE
  A MOTHER GOOSE BOOK
  FINGER manipulative toys

Safety Checklist

Toy safety testing is a voluntary practice, but reliable toy manufacturers consider it their responsibility to follow the tests and requirements set forth in their safety standard and know it makes good business sense to do so. In addition, the U.S. Consumer Products Safety Commission establishes and enforces Federal regulations regarding toy safety. Their toll-free phone number is (800) 638-2772.

Safety should be a factor from the *moment* a toy is *selected and purchased*. Keep this checklist of safety suggestions in mind when shopping for playthings:

☐ Use recommended age labeling as a guide and look for warnings and other safety messages on toy packaging.

☐ Consider the home environment and other, possibly younger, children who may be there. A plaything intended for an older child may be unsuitable and potentially dangerous in the hands of younger siblings (more about this when we discuss storage and supervision).

☐ Especially when buying for children under the age of three, avoid toys with small parts that could be ingested; those with sharp points and edges that could be hazardous. (The TMA Safety Standard includes requirements for testing toys which are intended for children under three years of age for small parts, "rolled" edges and sharp points.)

☐ Check for sturdy, well-sewn seams on stuffed animals and cloth dolls. Be certain eyes and noses on such items are securely fastened and cannot be pulled or bitten off.

☐ Make certain that rubber rattles, squeakers and teething toys are too large to fit completely in an infant's mouth. In addition, check to see that once a rubber toy is in its most compressed state, it is still too large to fit into baby's mouth.

☐ Electric toys with heating elements are appropriate for youngsters *over* eight years old, *as long as there is adult supervision.*

☐ Arrows and darts used by children should have blunt tips such as rubber or flexible plastic suction cups, cork or other protective points. Be certain the tips are attached securely to their shafts.

☐ Look for the words "non-toxic" on painted toys; "flame retardant/flame resistant" on fabrics; "machine/surface washable" on stuffed and cloth toys; and "UL Approved" for Underwriters Laboratories on electrical playthings.

☐ Choose a toy storage chest that has a removable lid or a hinged lid that will *remain securely open*. If you select a wooden toy chest, check for smooth finished edges and one with proper holes for ventilation and hinge line clearances to prevent pinched fingers.

©Toy Manufacturers of America

Toy Manufacturers

Brio Toys (and Corolle)
Brio Scanditoy Corporation
6531 N. Sidney Place
Milwaukee, WI 53209

Chicco (Kee-ko)
Artsana of America
200 Fifth Avenue
New York, NY 10010

Childcraft
(Retail stores and catalog)
Childcraft Education Corp.
20 Kilmer Road
Edison, NJ 08818

Child Guidance/Wonder Toys
CBS Toys
41 Madison Avenue
New York, NY 10010

Childwork (Catalog)
Family Bazaar
352 Evelyn Street
Paramus, NJ 07652

Crayola
Binney & Smith, Inc.
1100 Church Lane
Easton, PA 18042

Discovery Toys (Catalog)
4650 East Second Street
Benicia, CA 94510

Eden Toys
112 West 34th Street
New York, NY 10020

Dollsanddreams
454 Third Avenue
New York, NY 10016

F.A.O. Schwarz
(Retail stores and catalog)
Fifth Avenue at 58th Street
New York, NY 10151

The First Years toys
(see Kiddie Products)

Fischerform
Fischer America, Inc.
14-20 Madison Road
Fairfield, NJ 07006

Fisher-Price Toys
636 Girard Avenue
East Aurora, NY 14052

Freemountain Toys, Inc.
23 Main Street
Bristol, VT 05443

Galt Toys (and Ladybird books)
60 Church Street – Yalesville
Wallingford, CT 06492

Gund, Inc.
44 National Road
Edison, NJ 08817

International Playthings
151 Forest Street
Montclair, NJ 07042
(Brima, Berchet, HP Toys.
Kiddicraft)

Johnson & Johnson
Child Development Center
Skillman, NJ 08558

Kiddie Products, Inc.
One Kiddie Drive
Avon, MA 02322

LEGO Toys and DUPLO Toys
LEGO Systems, Inc.
555 Taylor Road
Enfield, CT 06082

Little Tikes
8705 Freeway Drive
Macedonia, OH 44056

Playskool, Inc.
4501 West Augusta Boulevard
Chicago, IL 60651

Reeves International, Inc.
1007 Broadway
New York, NY 10010
(Kouvalias)

Scancraft
P. O. Box 220271
Charlotte, NC 28222
(Aarikka and Jukka toys)

Schowanek of America, Inc.
454 Third Avenue
New York, NY 10016

Shellcore, Inc.
3474 South Clinton Avenue
South Plainfield, NJ 07080

Small World Toys
P. O. Box 5291
Beverly Hills, CA 90210
(Acre, Ambi, Walter Wood,
Eichorn Wood Toys)

T. C. Timber
Habermaass Corp.
P. O. Box 42
Jordan Road
Skaneateles, NY 13152

TOMY Corp.
901 East 233rd Street
Carson, CA 90749

Toys That Teach (catalog)
(see Childcraft)

Toys To Grow On (catalog)
P. O. Box 17
Long Beach, CA 90801

Tupperware Home Parties
P. O. Box 2353
Orlando, FL 32802

Wonder Toys
CBS Toys
41 Madison Avenue
New York, NY 10010

BOOK PUBLISHERS

E. P. Dutton, Inc.
2 Park Avenue
New York, NY 10016

Golden Books
Western Publishing Co., Inc.
1220 Mound Avenue
Racine, WI 53404

Grosset and Dunlap
(see Putnam Publishing Group)

Houghton Mifflin Co.
One Beacon Street
Boston, MA 02108

Ladybird Books
Galt Toys
60 Church Street – Yalesville
Wallingford, CT 06492

Penguin Books
40 West 23rd Street
New York, NY 10010

Platt & Munk
(see Putnam Publishing Group)

Price/Stern/Sloan
410 North La Cienega Boulevard
Los Angeles, CA 90048

Putnam Publishing Group
200 Madison Avenue
New York, NY 10016

Rand McNally & Co.
8255 Central Park Avenue
Skokie, IL 60076

Random House
201 East 50th Street
New York, NY 10022

NOTE: *Most of the brand names cited are registered trademarks.*

Suggested Reading

Baby and Child Care, Benjamin Spock, M.D. (Pocket Books)

Babyhood, Penelope Leach (Knopf)

Babytalk: How Your Child Learns to Speak, M. Susan Beck (New American Library)

Better Homes and Gardens Baby Book (Bantam)

Complete Book of Children's Play, Ruth Hartley and Robert Goldenson (Crowell)

First Five Years of Life, Arnold Gesell, M.D. (Harper & Row)

First Three Years of Life, Burton L. White (Prentice-Hall)

First Twelve Months of Life—Your Baby's Growth Month by Month, Frank Caplan, general editor (Grosset & Dunlap)

First Wondrous Year, Richard A. Chase, M.D., Richard R. Rubin, Ph.D. (Johnson & Johnson Child Development Publications)

Good Things for Babies, Sandy Jones (Houghton-Mifflin)

How to Parent, Dr. Fitzhugh Dodson (New American Library)

How to Play With Your Baby, Athina Aston (East Woods Press)

How to Play With Your Children—And When Not To, Brian and Shirley Sutton-Smith (Hawthorne Books)

Infant and Child in the Culture of Today, Arnold Gesell, M.D. and Frances Ilg, M.D. (Harper & Row)

Infant Care (Children's Bureau, Department of Health, Education and Welfare, Washington, DC)

Infants and Mothers, Differences in Development, T. Berry Brazelton, M.D. (Delacorte Press)

Loving Hands—The Traditional Indian Art of Baby Massage, Dr. Frederick LeBoyer (Knopf)

Magic Years, Selma Fraiberg (Scribners)

Mothering, Rudolph Schaffer (Developing Child Series, Harvard University Press, Jerome Bruner, series editor)

Mothers Almanac, Marguerite Kelly and Ella Parsons (Doubleday)

New Parents' Guide to Early Learning, Sara Bennett Stein (New American Library)

Positive Parenting, Alvin N. Eden, M.D. (Bobbs-Merrill)

Power of Play, Frank and Theresa Caplan (Doubleday)

Second Twelve Months of Life, Frank and Theresa Caplan (Grosset & Dunlap)

Toys That Don't Care, Edward M. Schwartz (Gambit)

What Every Child Would Like His Parents to Know, Dr. Lee Salk (McKay)

Your Baby and Child, Penelope Leach (Knopf)

Your Child's Play, Arnold Arnold (Essandess)

MAGAZINES FOR PARENTS

Growing Child and Growing Parent, each monthly newsletter follows your child's development by birthdate, P. O. Box 620, Lafayette, IN 47902

Parents Magazine, available on the newsstand

Practical Parenting, excellent bimonthly newsletter edited by Vicki Lansky, 18326B Minnetonka Boulevard, Deephaven, MN 55391

Working Mother, available on the newsstand

Index

Index   128